DEDICATION

To my indomitable partner in life and love, my beautiful wife:
For your unwavering patience, for being the lighthouse amidst the storm, and for being the echo of laughter in my darkest nights, I extend my deepest gratitude. Your love has been my ink, your faith, my paper, and our shared dreams, my narrative. Thank you for walking this challenging, winding road alongside me. The chapters of this book, like our life together, bear the watermark of your love and support.

To my deceased parents, who were my backbone for far more than the 20 years this book has taken shape:
Your understanding and tolerance have been the bedrock on which I built my courage to dream and to write. Thank you for tolerating my endless tirades about chapter development and for believing in my journey even when the destination was out of sight.

To my sons:
You are my greatest creations.

This book is a testament to your love, support, and resilience. Without you, its pages would remain blank, its chapters unformed. Thank you for helping me turn a daunting twenty-year dream into a reality.

LENGTHEN YOUR STRIDE

The Power of 1% Improvements to Transform Your Life, Relationships, Career, Business, and the World

Uproar Media
Arlington, VA 22209
www.uprorr.com

A paperback edition is available as
ISBN: 979-8-9886038-4-9
A digital edition is available as
ISBN: 979-8-9886038-5-6
Library of Congress Control Number: 2023916011

LENGTHEN YOUR STRIDE
The Power of 1% Improvements to Transform Your Life, Relationships, Career, Business, and the World
by Bryant D. Nielson

LENGTHEN YOUR STRIDE

The Power of 1% Improvements to Transform Your Life, Relationships, Career, Business, and the World

BRYANT D NIELSON

ACKNOWLEDGMENTS

In the realm of dreams, ambitions, and realities, the inception of this book, "Lengthen Your Stride: The Power of 1% Improvements to Transform Your Life, Relationships, Career, Business, and the World," began as a seed of inspiration in the fertile soil of my youthful mind during the late 1970s.

A singular catalyst for this book, indeed for my entire life's trajectory, was Spencer W. Kimball. Through his influential concept of "Lengthen Your Stride," he challenged me and countless others to make continuous, small, and consistent improvements in our lives. His teaching served as a beacon, guiding my path toward a more purposeful existence. I owe much of the philosophy encapsulated within these pages to his wisdom.

The first draft of this book was born in the summer of 2003, an unknown ambition manifesting in the form of a humble outline. It was ambitious and promising, yet it lay dormant, slowly germinating over two decades. Now, after a journey of 20 years of countless moments of self-doubt and sprinkled with joyous revelations, it has come to fruition.

To my readers, I hope the lessons within these pages guide you to a deeper understanding of the power of small, consistent changes. As you turn each page, may you find the inspiration to lengthen your stride and, in so doing, transform your life and the world around you.

Thank you, from the deepest well of my gratitude, for joining me on this journey.

ABOUT THE AUTHOR

Bryant Nielson is more than a leading voice in the dynamic world of blockchain and cryptocurrency; he's a storyteller, a journeyman, and a patient architect of thought. His professional achievements are extensive, and while his role as the founder of the Web3 Certification Board, founder of The Blockchain Academy, and Chairman of the Government Blockchain Association stands as notable entries on his résumé, what truly sets Bryant apart is his passionate dedication to the art of learning and his commitment to the long, winding process of creating something meaningful and lasting.

The journey toward writing this book began decades ago. Each idea, every experience, and all the encounters along the way have been stepping stones, bringing Bryant closer to this goal. Much like the book, his career was not constructed overnight but was built slowly over time, shaped by a series of small, deliberate decisions and actions. This philosophy is embedded in his education approach and understanding of blockchain technology.

His writing reflects this patience and depth. Each article, blog post, and now, this book is a testament to his commitment to the slow, steady progression of ideas and the power of consistent, daily effort.

The long road to authorship has been marked by late nights of conversations, research, and an unwavering commitment to the journey. Through highs and lows, successes and setbacks, Bryant has shown that tenacity and perseverance are as valuable as knowledge and expertise.

Bryant is a true believer in the process of "Lengthen Your Stride;" his recent graduation with a Master's degree in Blockchain and Digital Currency from the University of Nicosia at age 64 underscores his commitment to lifelong learning and his dedication to understanding the nuances of disruptive technologies.

Bryant currently calls Arlington, Virginia, home, where he lives with his supportive wife. His journey continues, motivated by a relentless curiosity, a love for storytelling, and a dedication to innovation. As he looks forward, Bryant continues to explore, scribing his insights along the way, ever eager to share his journey with the world.

CONTENTS

FOREWORD

The first part of the book will introduce the overarching theme behind the "Lengthen Your Stride" concept and will delve into the transformative power of minor, incremental improvements. Personal stories and case studies will be shared to illustrate the potential impact of 1% improvements across various aspects of life.

CONCEPT OF "LENGTHEN YOUR STRIDE"

"Lengthen Your Stride" is a metaphor for making minor, incremental improvements in various aspects of your life to achieve lasting, transformative change. The idea is rooted in the belief that consistent, modest adjustments can compound over time, leading to significant personal and professional growth.

Rather than striving for radical changes or quick fixes, "Lengthen Your Stride" encourages individuals to make 1% improvements daily or consistently, allowing them to build positive habits, break negative ones, and develop resilience. This approach is more sustainable and achievable for most people and often leads to more meaningful, long-term results.

The concept can be applied to various areas of life, including personal development, relationships, career growth, business success, and positively impacting the world. By focusing on minor, achievable adjustments, individuals can gradually work toward their goals, minimize the risk of burnout, and ultimately create a better future for themselves and others.

IMPACT OF SMALL, INCREMENTAL IMPROVEMENTS

Minor, incremental improvements can profoundly impact various aspects of life when applied consistently over time. These modest changes, often called 1% improvements, can compound, leading to significant progress and transformation. The impact of such modifications can be seen in multiple areas, such as:

Personal Growth: By making minor adjustments in daily habits, individuals can develop new skills, enhance their knowledge, and cultivate a growth mindset. These improvements can increase self-confidence, resilience, and a sense of accomplishment.

Relationships: Small, consistent efforts in communication, understanding, and empathy can strengthen bonds and improve the quality of relationships. By investing in quality time and actively supporting the growth of loved ones, individuals can nurture deeper connections and a supportive network.

Career Advancement: Incremental improvements in skills, networking, and leadership abilities can increase job satisfaction, promotions, and new opportunities. Professionals can stay competitive and adapt to evolving market demands by focusing on continuous growth.

Business Success: In the business world, minor improvements in innovation, efficiency, and customer satisfaction can lead to increased revenue and growth. A culture of continuous improvement can help businesses stay agile, adapt to market changes, and maintain a competitive edge.

Global Impact: When individuals focus on incremental improvements in environmental sustainability and social responsibility, the collective impact can create positive change worldwide. By making mindful decisions, supporting eco-friendly initiatives, and advocating for ethical practices, we can contribute to a better world.

The impact of minor, incremental improvements lies in their compound effect over time. By embracing the "Lengthen Your Stride" philosophy and applying consistent 1% improvements, individuals can achieve meaningful, long-lasting growth and transformation in all areas of life.

PERSONAL OBSERVATIONS

OBSERVATION 1: EFFORT

Improving by 1% every day or every week can lead to significant growth and progress over time. The compounding effect of incremental improvements will result in substantial gains in various aspects of life, such as personal development, professional growth, relationships, and overall well-being.

If you improved by 1% every day: Over a year, this would mean improving by approximately 38 times (1.01^365 = 37.78). This means that by the end of the year, your performance or skill will be 38 times better than when you started. This exponential growth showcases the power of daily incremental improvements.

If you improved by 1% every week: Over a year (52 weeks), this would mean improving by approximately 68% (1.01^52 = 1.682). This translates to an increase in performance or skill by more than two-thirds of your starting point. Although the growth is less dramatic than daily improvements, it is still substantial and can lead to significant progress.

It is essential to note that maintaining consistent 1% improvement might be challenging in reality, as progress tends to ebb and flow. However, striving for minor, constant improvements can lead to lasting positive changes in various aspects of life.

OBSERVATION 2: READING

The number of minutes per day needed to read 25 books in a year depends on your reading speed and the average length of the books you're reading. Let's assume the average book length is about 300 pages, a standard size for many novels and non-fiction books.

Calculate the total number of pages you need to read for 25 books:

25 books * 300 pages/book = 7,500 pages

Determine the number of days in a year:

365 days

Calculate the number of pages you need to read per day:

7,500 pages / 365 days ≈ 20.55 pages/day

Now, let's assume that your reading speed is about 200 words per minute, an average reading speed for adults. Additionally, let's take that there are about 250 words per page.

Calculate the number of words you need to read per day:

20.55 pages/day * 250 words/page ≈ 5,137.5 words/day

Determine the number of minutes you need to read per day:

5,137.5 words/day / 200 words/minute ≈ 25.69 minutes/day

So, to read 25 books of 300 pages each in a year, you would need to read for approximately 25.69 minutes per day, assuming an average reading speed of 200 words per minute. That is less than half the length of most Netflix series episodes. Instead of watching three episodes every night, watching two will give you ample time to consume these books.

Reading 25 books a year can develop and improve various skills and knowledge, depending on the book's subjects and genres. Here are some potential skills you might develop by reading 25 books a year:

Improved Vocabulary and Language Skills: Reading regularly can expand your vocabulary, improve grammar, and better understand language nuances.

Enhanced Comprehension and Critical Thinking: Reading different types of books helps sharpen your ability to understand complex ideas, analyze information, and develop logical arguments.

Broader General Knowledge: Reading books on various topics, such as history, science, or art, can increase your general knowledge and make you more well-rounded.

Better Communication Skills: Reading books, especially those on communication and interpersonal skills, can improve your ability to interact with others, listen effectively, and express your thoughts clearly.

Increased Empathy and Emotional Intelligence: Reading fiction can help you understand different perspectives and emotions, leading to increased empathy and emotional intelligence.

Greater Creativity and Imagination: Reading books, particularly fiction, and literature, can spark your creativity and develop your imagination by exposing you to new ideas, worlds, and characters.

Enhanced Problem-Solving Skills: Reading books on various subjects can provide you with different approaches to problem-solving, decision-making, and critical thinking, which can be applied in real-life situations.

Personal and Professional Development: Reading books on personal growth, self-improvement, and career development can help you acquire new skills, learn about your strengths and weaknesses, and set and achieve your goals.

By reading 25 books a year, you can continuously develop and enhance these skills, leading to personal growth and improved performance in various aspects of life, including work, relationships, and overall well-being.

OBSERVATION 3: GOLF

The 2022 U.S. Open occurred at The Country Club in Brookline, Massachusetts. The final standings were as follows:

1st Place: Matt Fitzpatrick - 6 under par (274 total strokes)

2nd Place: Scottie Scheffler and Will Zalatoris - both with five under par (275 full strokes)

The difference between 1st and 2nd places in 2020 was six strokes or a difference of 0.0214%

Four golfers shared the 10th place in the 2022 U.S. Open at even par (280 total strokes). The difference between 1st and 10th place was six strokes or a difference of 0.0420%.

The 2021 U.S. Open occurred at Torrey Pines Golf Course in San Diego, California. The final standings were as follows:

1st Place: Jon Rahm - 6 under par (278 total strokes)

2nd Place: Louis Oosthuizen - 5 under par (279 full strokes)

The difference between 1st and 2nd places in 2021 was one stroke or a difference of 0.00358%.

The 10th place in the 2021 U.S. Open was shared by five golfers at one under par (283 total strokes). The difference between 1st place and 10th place was five strokes or a difference of 0.0177%

What was the difference in winnings for each finisher in the tournament?

For the 2022 U.S. Open, the prize money distribution was as follows:

1st place: Matt Fitzpatrick - $3,150,000

2nd place: Scottie Scheffler and Will Zalatoris both received - $1,890,000

The difference in winnings between 1st and 2nd place in 2022 was $1,260,000 or 40% less for the second-place finisher.

The 10th-place finisher in the 2022 U.S. Open received $425,830.

The difference in winnings between 1st and 10th place was approximately $2,724,170 or roughly 86.48% less for the 10th place finisher.

For the 2021 U.S. Open, the prize money distribution was as follows:

1st Place: Jon Rahm - $2,250,000

2nd Place: Louis Oosthuizen - $1,350,000

The difference in winnings between 1st and 2nd place in 2021 was $900,000 or 39.91% less for the second-place finisher.

The 10th-place finishers in the 2021 U.S. Open each received $366,058.33, as the total prize for the 10th place ($1,830,291.65) was divided among the five players who tied for the position.

The difference in winnings between 1st and 10th place was approximately $1,883,941.67 or roughly 83.73% less for the 10th-place finisher.

OBSERVATION 4: F1 RACING

Formula 1 races are held at various circuits worldwide, and finishing times vary depending on the specific race. Therefore, let's consider the 2020 Abu Dhabi Grand Prix and the 2021 Bahrain Grand Prix:

2022 Abu Dhabi Grand Prix:

1st Place: Max Verstappen (Red Bull Racing) - 1:27:45.914

2nd Place: Charles Leclerc (Ferrari) - 1:36:35.402, a difference of 0.00104% (+8.771)

10th Place: Lando Norris (McLaren) - 1:37:25.542, a difference of 0.00975% (83.898)

2021 Bahrain Grand Prix:

1st Place: Lewis Hamilton (Mercedes) - 1:32:03.897

2nd Place: Max Verstappen (Red Bull Racing) - 1:32:04.432, a difference of 0.00018%

10th Place: Lance Stroll (Aston Martin) - 1:32:37.764, a difference of 0.00612%

In life, minor differences in outcomes can often lead to significant disparities in rewards, as evidenced by the worlds of reading, golf, and Formula 1 racing. A consistent reading practice, for instance, can result in minor incremental improvements in vocabulary and comprehension that translate into substantial personal and professional growth. Similarly, golfers who consistently refine their skills can experience remarkable differences in rankings, prize money, and career opportunities, even by a stroke or two.

In the high-stakes realm of Formula 1 racing, a split-second advantage in finishing times can determine the difference between victory and defeat, profoundly impacting team standings, sponsorships, and the drivers' careers. These examples illustrate the power of marginal gains and how minor, consistent improvements can accumulate over time, ultimately leading to significant rewards and success.

OBSERVATIONS 5: OLYMPICS

The Olympics are full of examples of where minor incremental improvements resulted in dominating the respective fields. I could have chosen anything from Swimming, Track and Field, and Cycling to make this point. The example I will share is about the men's triathlon in the Tokyo 2020 Olympics, which took place in July 2021 and consists of swimming, cycling, and running without stopping between events. The competition is a test of endurance, strength, and speed.

The results of the men's triathlon at the Tokyo 2020 Olympics were:

Gold: Kristian Blummenfelt, from Norway, with a time of 1:45:04

Silver: Alex Yee, from Great Britain, with a time of 1:45:15, a difference of 0.174% (11 seconds)

10th Place: Mario Mola, from Spain, with a time of 1:46:13, a difference of 1.095% (69 seconds) from the gold medalist's time.

These athletes showcased their endurance, strength, and speed throughout the race, demonstrating their exceptional abilities in the challenging triathlon event. However, the difference between the Gold and 10th finishers was 1% or less. Let us consider these numbers: the difference between the gold and silver place finishers was 11 seconds, which amounted to less than two-tenths of 1 percent. The difference between the gold and the 10th place finisher was 69 seconds, or just a hair over 1 percent difference. That 1 percent outcome makes all of the difference in the world.

In life, minor differences in outcomes can often lead to significant disparities in rewards, as evidenced by the worlds of reading, golf, the Olympics, and Formula 1 racing.

These examples illustrate the power of marginal gains and how minor, consistent improvements can accumulate over time, ultimately leading to significant rewards and success.

PART 1

PERSONAL TRANSFORMATION

CHAPTER ONE

THE POWER OF HABITS

Do you want to know about the psychology of habits, their role in our lives, and how they influence our actions? Are you interested in learning about the approaches to help you create positive habits, break negative ones, and maintain consistency to attain long-term growth? If so, we must start by understanding habits!

UNDERSTANDING HABITS AND THEIR ROLE IN OUR LIVES

Ever wondered what role habits play in our everyday lives? We may not realize it, but unconsciously, our habits become a part of us.

Let's take this as an example. Tying shoes requires effort. As you keep practicing, learning this skill becomes a process that eventually becomes familiar, something you don't need mental effort to do. You just do it based on your muscle memory.[1] After some time, the repeated actions become 'habits.'

> *"We are what we repeatedly do. Excellence, then, is not an act but a habit."*
>
> —Aristotle

THE PSYCHOLOGICAL AND NEUROLOGICAL BASIS OF HABITS

Whether we realize it or not, habits become a part of our everyday lives. But it's not that easy to form habits—certain psychological and neurological factors are involved. Habituation is a process by which our brains link certain behaviors or actions with specific environmental cues or stimuli.

As for the psychological aspect of habits, when we repetitively perform a behavior in response to a particular cue, our brain learns to associate that behavior with that cue, and the behavior becomes a habit. An example would be this: if we check our phones regularly whenever we receive a notification, our brain learns to associate the sound with this particular behavior.

Habits also have a neurological basis that relates to the biological makeup of our existence. It involves the functioning of the brain. On a neurological level, our cerebrum releases dopamine, a synapse that builds up the way of behavior. Over the period, these associations become more programmed.

If we are to talk about habit formation in more formal terms, it depends on the basal ganglia, a group of structures that lie

1 https://positivepsychology.com/how-habits-are-formed/

deep within our brains. These structures coordinate voluntary movements, such as walking, talking, eating, and running. You perform them daily but need to realize what part of your brain is helping you complete these actions.

While basal ganglia support all these daily actions, the prefrontal cortex controls goal-directed behavior and decision-making. And then there's the sensory cortex, which is responsible for sensing environmental cues. Now, why are the prefrontal cortex and sensory cortex critical? They provide input to the basal ganglia and indirectly impact habit formation. When a way of behaving becomes a habit, the basal ganglia start acting naturally, without conscious effort from the prefrontal cortex.

ANALYZING HOW HABITS SHAPE OUR PERSONALITY AND IDENTITY

Habits can influence our personality and character by affecting how we think, feel, and act on a daily basis. If we allow bad habits to control us, our personalities will be negatively impacted. On the other hand, if we have good habits, we become prone to having a good personality. Therefore, we can say that the collection of our habits makes up our character and mirrors our qualities and needs throughout everyday life.

Additionally, habits can contribute to our overall sense of identity by creating a sense of consistency in our everyday lives. Our habits foster willpower and self-discipline, which make us capable of reaching our objectives when we successfully form healthy habits.

Have you ever wondered how we can become the best version of ourselves and positively shape our personality and identity? This can be done by intentionally breaking bad habits and forming good ones.

ASSESSING THE CUMULATIVE EFFECT OF HABITS ON OVERALL WELL-BEING AND LIFE SATISFACTION

Since habits play a role in our everyday lives and shape our personalities, we can say that they impact our well-being and life satisfaction. Good habits can lead to an improvement in our well-being. Better mental and physical health and increased happiness and productivity can result from developing healthy habits and breaking bad ones.

By adopting healthy lifestyle choices like eating a well-balanced diet, regular exercise, getting enough sleep, and staying away from harmful substances, your physical health and overall sense of fulfillment and well-being will improve.

Furthermore, spending time with loved ones, practicing mindfulness, engaging in hobbies, and reducing stress can all contribute to better mental health.

Increased productivity can lead to a sense of accomplishment, which can be achieved by prioritizing tasks, setting goals, and avoiding distractions. We can achieve life satisfaction and greater happiness through practices like engaging in positive self-talk, practicing gratitude, and cultivating positive relationships.

RECOGNIZING THE INFLUENCE OF HABITS ON OUR DAILY ACTIONS AND CHOICES

Habits can drive our decision-making processes by automating particular actions and responses. When we form a routine, it becomes a habit that we carry out unconsciously. We free up our mental capacity by automatically making decisions. By giving ourselves more mental space, we can utilize that intellectual ability for thinking. Our habits can impact our decisions frequently, and we need to understand them. Let's enlighten you on how habits affect our decision-making processes.

Habits provide a default response that we choose with little thought when faced with a decision. Let's give you an example. Every morning when you wake up, instead of deciding whether or not to exercise, you might choose to go for a run when you wake up every morning because you are accustomed to doing so. This is a default response. You may not even realize this. This is also one-way habits play a role in our lives.

In addition, our desires and preferences can have an impact on the choices we make because of our routines. For example, if we regularly consume healthy foods, we might naturally select healthier options.

> *"Chains of habits are too light to be felt until they are too heavy to be broken."*
>
> —Warren Buffet

NOTICING THE ROLE OF HABITS IN TIME MANAGEMENT AND PRODUCTIVITY

If you see, you will realize that you can accomplish a lot in less period by developing good habits that allow you to complete tasks more quickly and with less effort. Habits are essential to effective time management and productivity because they enable us to use our time better and automate our routines.

For example, if we check our email first thing in the morning, we can quickly take care of urgent messages and move on to more pressing matters.

Our lives are more predictable and structured when we follow a routine. We can better plan our time when we have a way because we know what to expect. When it comes to productivity and time management, consistency is essential. Habits assist us with remaining steady with our assignments and day-to-day schedules, which can prompt better progress after some time.

Moreover, we can increase productivity and time management by consciously changing bad habits with good ones. For instance, if procrastination is a bad habit for us, we can change it by dividing tasks into smaller, more manageable chunks that can be completed over time.

ACKNOWLEDGING HOW HABITS IMPACT OUR RELATIONSHIPS AND INTERACTIONS WITH OTHERS

Have you ever wondered how habits can affect how we socialize with others? How do we behave in relationships, how do we communicate, and how do we form connections and build trust with others? In the following ways, our habits can affect relationships and interactions with others.

1. *Our communication habits can influence the way we tend to interact with others. For instance, engaging in active listening daily may indicate a better level of interest and engagement in the conversation. This will make the other person feel heard and show that you are understanding.*

2. *Keeping promises, being punctual, and showing appreciation are all examples of good habits that can strengthen relationships and build trust.*

3. *Empathy, support, and kindness are good habits that can improve our relationships and interactions with others. Negative behaviors like being critical, judgmental, or dismissive can drive people away and damage our relationships.*

IDENTIFYING THE HABIT LOOP: CUE, ROUTINE, AND REWARD

What is a habit loop? What stages does it have? Charles Duhigg says that the brain needs a precise beginning and ending point for a habit to become automatic in different situations. These points help the formation of a habit loop. Let's make it simple for you by clarifying how Duhigg points out the three essential factors that help the brain in making these points.

To begin, there is the **cue**, a trigger that sets the habit in motion and forces the brain into automatic mode. Cues can come in many different ways, including physical places, times of day, feelings, people, previous actions, and sensory stimuli like smells and sounds. For instance, a cell phone's buzzing can force us to check our messages.

Second is the **routine**, the set of behaviors or actions the brain has stored for that habit.

Last but not least, there is the **reward**, which signifies the end of the habit and is the result of the routine.

The **cues** will set the habits that will form a **routine**. The last stage of the loop is the **reward**. This will motivate you to adopt good habits because you know you will gain.

ACKNOWLEDGING THE LONG-TERM IMPACT OF HABITS ON PERSONAL AND PROFESSIONAL SUCCESS

RECOGNIZING THE CORRELATION BETWEEN HABIT FORMATION AND ACHIEVING GOALS

Habit formation and achieving goals are closely interrelated. Habits can be a powerful tool for achieving goals because they help to automate behaviors and make them easier to execute consistently over time. By developing habits that align with our goals, we can progress toward them daily and increase our chances of success. If you want to live a successful life, the first thing you need to do is to adopt good habits.

EVALUATING THE ROLE OF HABITS IN MAINTAINING WORK-LIFE BALANCE AND REDUCING STRESS

Do you need help managing your work with your personal life? Does a hectic work routine stress you out? Habits can play an essential role in maintaining work-life balance and reducing stress. Instead of fretting about it, go through the few ways in which your good habits will contribute to a healthy work-life balance and reduce your stress:

Prioritization: Habits can help us prioritize our energy and time, which is critical for maintaining work-life balance. Learning how to prioritize work and personal life to have a work-life balance would be best.

Boundaries: Habits can help us set boundaries between personal and work life, reducing stress and improving overall well-being. For example, developing a habit of not checking work emails outside of work hours can create a clear boundary between personal time and work, reducing the stress and anxiety that comes with it.

Self-care: Your good habits will lead to self-care, which is critical for overall well-being. You should develop healthy eating, exercise, sleep, and relaxation habits to help you reduce stress and improve your mental and physical health.

Time management: Managing time is essential in your professional life. Many people complain about increased workload and stress at work. Habits can support effective time management, reducing stress, and improving work-life balance. You can use a time-tracking tool or set daily priorities to reduce the stress of feeling overworked or overwhelmed.

CREATING POSITIVE HABITS THROUGH 1% IMPROVEMENTS

"Small daily improvements are the key to staggering long-term results."

They say you need to start with baby steps if you want to achieve something big. This means creating positive habits through marginal changes to your habits to gradually improve the overall behavior that will make you successful. These minor adjustments might seem trivial and unimportant at first, but if you look back, you will realize that they have contributed to significant improvements in life.

For example, if your goal is to exercise regularly, you could start with small, achievable goals like taking a 10-minute walk every day instead of trying to go from no exercise to a rigorous daily routine. As these small changes become habits, you can gradually increase the time and intensity of your exercise routine.

Likewise, if you want to eat healthier, you could start by making small changes like reducing your sugar intake or incorporating more vegetables into your meals. Over time, these small changes can lead to an essential improvement in your overall diet.

Creating positive habits through marginal changes is to focus on making small, sustainable changes you can maintain over time. By gradually improving your habits, you can attain long-term success in achieving your goals.

The Kaizen approach is a philosophy that stresses the importance of continuous improvement through small, incremental changes. It originated in Japan and has been widely accepted in healthcare and manufacturing industries. The Kaizen approach is based on the concept that continuous improvement is vital in attaining excellent results. This means constantly looking for ways to improve processes, products, and services through small changes. This approach emphasizes improving processes rather than just outcomes. By improving processes, better results can be achieved more efficiently and consistently.

Organizations can achieve continuous improvement and better results over time by adopting the Kaizen approach. This approach emphasizes small, incremental changes that can be easily implemented rather than significant changes that can be hard to execute.

SETTING ACHIEVABLE AND REALISTIC GOALS TO FOSTER HABIT FORMATION

UTILIZING THE SMART GOAL-SETTING FRAMEWORK

When you set big goals for yourself, it can get intimidating. However, the challenges should not hold you back from pursuing your dreams. If you set realistic targets for yourself to achieve your goals, you can achieve anything.

Do you know about the SMART goal-setting technique? It is a common approach for setting explicit, quantifiable, attainable, pertinent, and time-bound goals. You have yet to learn how beneficial it is. To make you understand better, we have provided a breakdown of what every one of these parts implies:

1. **Specific**. This implies that you should characterize the exact thing you need to accomplish.

2. **Measurable:** Your goal should be measurable to track progress and determine success. You can establish specific metrics or milestones that will enable you to monitor progress toward the goal.

3. **Achievable:** The goal should be attainable, given the available resources and constraints.

4. **Relevant:** The goal should be related to your overall goals and priorities. As a result, you should choose a goal that aligns with your personal or professional goals and values.

5. **Time-bound:** The goal should be time-bound, with a particular cutoff time or course of events for fulfillment. This implies that one should set a specific date by which the goal can be accomplished.

Using the SMART goal-setting framework, you can set more attainable, measurable objectives that are more likely to be met. You can use this framework to stay focused on your goals, keep track of your progress toward your goals, and adjust your strategy as needed to ensure you are moving forward. Whether aiming for personal or professional success, the SMART framework should be your go-to tool.

BREAKING DOWN LONG-TERM GOALS INTO SMALLER, SHORT-TERM OBJECTIVES

It is essential to divide your long-term goals into smaller, more manageable goals. There is no harm in dreaming big and thinking about where you wish to be in the next few years. However, it would be best if you broke them down into short-term goals so that they seem realistic. Here are a few stages that you can follow:

Begin by determining your long-term objective: List your long-term goals. For example, write down your long-term aim of learning a new language.

Characterize the events: Choose a time frame for achieving your long-term objective. This will give you a thought of the number of targets you need to set.

Separate the drawn-out objective into more modest targets: Divide your long-term objective into smaller ones. These goals should be explicit, quantifiable, attainable, significant, and time-bound. You could set a short-term objective of learning 100 new words within the first month if your long-term objective is to become fluent in a new language in a few years.

Set priorities for the goals: Prioritize the short-term goals on your list in order of importance and urgency.

Make an activity plan: Create a strategy for each short-term goal. Set deadlines for each step and the steps you must take to reach each goal.

Monitor your progress: Monitor your progress toward your short-term goals regularly. Reevaluate your action plan and make any necessary adjustments if you discover that you are falling behind.

APPLYING THE CONCEPT OF MARGINAL GAINS TO DAILY ROUTINES

Following are several ways you can bring slight changes to your routine:

- *Divide tasks into manageable steps: Break down a problem area into manageable chunks. For instance, if you want to start meditating daily, start with just ten minutes and gradually increase the amount of time you spend doing it.*

- *Monitor your progress: Celebrate small victories and keep track of your progress. It would be best if you were your cheerleader.*
- *Always evaluate and adjust: Reevaluate your routine consistently and change your methodology as needed. Adaptability and adjusting as required are essential because some changes may work better.*

Applying marginal gains to daily routines might include taking a short walk during a break from work, setting a timer to limit time spent on social media, or stretching for a few minutes in the morning. Although these minor adjustments may appear irrelevant on their own, they can significantly enhance overall well-being and productivity when taken together over time.

TRACKING PROGRESS AND CELEBRATING SMALL WINS TO MAINTAIN MOTIVATION

Do you need help staying motivated? Is tracking your goals making you feel stressed out? No need to be! Habit-tracking tools and techniques can effectively track your progress toward achieving your goals and staying motivated by celebrating small wins. Here are some tips for utilizing habit-tracking tools and techniques to track small wins for motivation.

Use an app that tracks routines: You can easily track your progress toward your goals with various habit-tracking apps. Habitica, Streaks, and Loop Habit Tracker are among the most well-liked choices. You can often track your progress over time, get help setting goals, and get reminders from these apps.

Choose actions that matter: Choose routines that mean a lot to you and are essential to you. Staying motivated and appreciating small victories will be made more accessible by this.

Begin small: Start with simple, doable routines to track and stick to. This will assist you in gaining momentum and make it simpler to maintain your routine over time.

Set updates: You can set reminders on your computer or phone to remind you to follow your routines or track your progress.

Recognize small victories: Celebrate the little successes along the way. This will help you remain motivated and emphasize the significance of your routines. You can acknowledge your progress and give yourself a mental pat on the back as a reward, or you can reward yourself with something small like a favorite snack or a relaxing activity.

Monitor progress: Celebrate when you reach milestones and keep track of your progress over time. You can see how far you've come toward your goals, which can motivate you.

ESTABLISHING A REWARD SYSTEM FOR POSITIVE REINFORCEMENT

How does it feel when someone praises you or rewards you for something you have accomplished? The feeling is excellent. Positive reinforcement and motivation can be effectively achieved by implementing a reward system. So, how can you develop an effective reward system? No need to fear as we have provided you with some useful tips below:

Set clear goals: Begin by setting specific goals for yourself. These goals should be specific, measurable, and doable. For instance, if you want to practice more, put forth an objective to practice for 30 minutes daily, three times weekly.

Choose the right rewards: If you love coffee, for instance, you could give yourself a latte from your favorite coffee shop as a reward for reaching your weekly exercise goal.

Measuring points: Set rewards for achieving your goals by breaking them down into smaller milestones. For instance, if you want to write a book, you might offer a reward for finishing the first chapter.

Make it challenging but doable: Make goals that are difficult but doable. The reward may only be as meaningful if the goal is easy enough. If it's excessively troublesome, you might feel deterred and lose inspiration.

Monitor progress: Reward yourself when you reach each milestone and keep track of your progress toward your goals. You'll be able to stay motivated and reinforce good behavior with this.

BREAKING NEGATIVE HABITS WITH SMALL CHANGES

A crucial step in breaking bad habits and starting new, healthier ones is determining their patterns and root causes. The question is, how to break bad habits? Like always, we have provided you with some tips on how to go about it!

Determine the behavior: Begin by identifying the habit you need to change. This could be anything from putting off essential tasks to biting your nails.

Be aware of triggers: Watch for the things that set off the habit. Environmental (such as a specific location or time), emotional (such as boredom or stress), or social (such as being around particular people) triggers are all examples of triggers.

Identify the goal: Find out what the habit does for you. Habits frequently serve a purpose, such as reducing anxiety or providing comfort. If you know the goal, you can find other actions that can accomplish the same thing.

Consider the effects of the habit: What impact does the routine have on your life? Does it affect your relationships or goals? You can be motivated to change by knowing what will happen.

Seek assistance: Finally, if you need it, get help. Getting help from friends, family, or a therapist can be helpful when breaking a habit.

IMPLEMENTING GRADUAL MODIFICATIONS TO DISRUPT NEGATIVE HABIT LOOPS

It's always baby steps! Are you trying to disrupt negative habit loops and establish new, healthier habits? We can assure you that it can be done quickly by following the steps mentioned below:

Begin small: Start by making minor adjustments to your routine. For instance, to begin practicing more, start with only 10 minutes daily instead of jumping into an entire exercise routine every practice.

Identify the causes: Determine the factors that set off your lousy habit cycle. For instance, assuming you will often bite your tongue when worried, recognize the circumstances or sentiments that trigger that behavior.

Change the way you act: Substitute the bad habit with another positive mechanism, such as going for a stroll when you are worried or anxious.

Monitor progress: You should celebrate small victories and keep track of your progress. You'll be able to stay motivated and reinforce good behavior with this.

Repetition of the new action: You should keep practicing the new behavior. Be patient and persistent because this can take several months to complete.

ESTABLISHING NEW ROUTINES TO REPLACE AND COUNTERACT NEGATIVE HABITS

By establishing new routines, you can replace negative habits with positive behaviors with the same purpose. Over time, these new routines can become healthy habits that support your overall well-being.

An excellent way to get rid of bad habits is to start new routines, and if you need help with that, here are some tips:

Determine the bad habit: The first step is identifying the bad habit you want to eliminate. This could be anything from delaying to smoking.

Determine the goal: Find out what the bad habit is used for. Habits frequently serve a purpose, such as reducing anxiety or providing comfort. If you know the goal, you can find other actions that can accomplish the same thing.

Find new ways to act: Find new habits that can replace the bad habits.

Establish a routine: Establish a routine based on the new behavior. For instance, if you want to exercise more, set aside 30 minutes each morning before work.

Keep your word: Consistency is vital. Maintain the daily routine until it becomes a habit. Be patient and persistent because this can take several months to complete.

Screen progress: Celebrate small victories and keep track of your progress. You'll be able to stay motivated and reinforce good behavior with this.

STAYING CONSISTENT AND OVERCOMING SETBACKS

ACKNOWLEDGING THE IMPORTANCE OF PERSISTENCE IN HABIT FORMATION

YOU MIGHT HAVE HEARD THE PHRASE THAT PATIENCE BEARS ITS fruit. Persistence is an essential element in habit formation. Building a new habit is difficult; it requires persistent and consistent effort over time. It takes consistency, time, and effort to create a new habit, and persistence is vital to maintain the behavior until it becomes automatic. You can stay motivated and committed to building healthy new habits.

EMBRACING FAILURE AS A LEARNING OPPORTUNITY AND STEPPING STONE TO SUCCESS

What happens when you fail at something that you want to achieve? It feels like the end of the world, right? We are here to tell you that embracing failure as a learning opportunity and stepping stone to success is a powerful mindset shift that can assist you in achieving your goals and building resilience.

It encourages you to take risks. It acknowledges that failure is a natural part of the learning process and that you learn from your mistakes. Moreover, it helps to build resilience. It teaches you to adapt to change, bounce back from setbacks, and persevere in facing challenges. Failure serves as a learning opportunity and helps you learn from your mistakes and grow. It encourages continuous improvement, self-reflection, and problem-solving.

Embracing failure reduces fear and anxiety around taking risks. It acknowledges that failure is a natural part of the process and that there is always an opportunity to grow. Furthermore, it supports creativity and innovation as it encourages you to think outside the box, take risks, and try new approaches to problem-solving.

EMBRACING THE IMPORTANCE OF CONSISTENCY IN HABIT FORMATION AND GROWTH

You might have heard the phrase – *consistency is the key!* We assure you that it is critical to ingrain new habits. Through repetition, behaviors become automatic responses ingrained in our daily routines. To motivate you, we have mentioned a few reasons why consistency is crucial in habit formation:

1. *When we repeat a behavior repeatedly, we strengthen the neural pathways associated with that behavior. This makes the behavior more straightforward to perform and more automatic over time.*

2. *Consistency helps to build momentum in habit formation. Each time we engage in a new behavior, we reinforce the habit, making it easier to perform it again.*

3. *Repetition can help to overcome resistance to change. When you repeatedly engage in new behavior, you become more comfortable, making it easier to stick to the habit, even when challenging or inconvenient.*

ENCOURAGING PATIENCE AND PERSEVERANCE THROUGH INEVITABLE SETBACKS

"Never give up. Today is hard, tomorrow will be worse, but the day after tomorrow will be sunshine."

—Jack Mao

As mentioned, encouraging patience and perseverance through inevitable setbacks is essential for long-term success and personal growth. It may seem that your world is ending, but that's a life cycle. It would be best if you faced all the hardships with tenacity, and here are some reasons why:

Acknowledges setbacks as part of the process: Encouraging patience and perseverance acknowledges that setbacks are inevitable in any journey toward success. It helps you to view challenges and obstacles as opportunities for growth and learning.

Promotes resilience: Encouraging patience and perseverance fosters resilience. It teaches you to bounce back from setbacks and to keep going, even when things get tough.

Supports long-term commitment: Encouraging patience and perseverance supports long-term commitment. It helps you to stay focused on your goals, even when progress is slow or difficult.

Cultivates self-discipline: Encouraging patience and perseverance cultivates self-discipline. It teaches you to stay committed to your goals and to persevere even when you don't feel like it.

Builds self-confidence: Encouraging patience and perseverance builds self-confidence. It helps you to believe in yourself and your abilities, even in the face of setbacks or failures.

PRACTICING SELF-COMPASSION AND MAINTAINING A POSITIVE OUTLOOK ON SETBACKS

You are a warrior – always remember that! Practicing self-compassion and maintaining a positive mindset during struggles is essential for your mental and emotional well-being. Love yourself and prioritize your mental health.

You need to practice self-compassion so that stress and anxiety can be reduced. It encourages a more upbeat and supportive inner dialogue and helps to combat negative self-talk. It enables you to recognize and respond constructively and positively to your feelings.

Self-compassion and maintaining a positive attitude in the face of setbacks boost self-esteem. It enables you to feel good about yourself even in the face of setbacks or failures by helping you to acknowledge your accomplishments and strengths.

It enables you to recognize setbacks as opportunities for growth and learning and allows you to learn from your mistakes.

ACTIVELY SEEKING OUT NEW CHALLENGES AND OPPORTUNITIES FOR GROWTH

You should always embark on new challenges and push yourself outside of your comfort zone, which can improve your sense of self-efficacy. Effectively searching out new difficulties helps you to become the best version of yourself. It enables you to fulfill your ambitions and realize your full potential. You can continuously grow and reach your full potential if you actively seek new challenges and opportunities for development.

CHAPTER TWO

BUILDING RESILIENCE

Have you ever felt the weight of hardships on your shoulders? Have you ever thought that the trouble you are going through is never-ending? It happens to the best of us.

Life doesn't come with a map—the harsh reality is that everyone has to experience twists and turns. From everyday challenges to traumatic events with long-lasting impacts like a severe illness, the death of a loved one, or a life-changing accident, each change has a different effect on people, bringing a unique flood of thoughts and strong emotions.

Despite this, people typically adapt well over time to life-altering, stressful situations—all thanks to resilience.

Instead of giving up on yourself and life, you must build resilience and remain steadfast despite obstacles. The quote from Rocky Balboa magnificently describes how people should keep going forward when life gives them lemons.

> *"It's not about how hard you hit; it's about how hard you can get hit and keep moving forward."*
>
> —Rocky Balboa

Psychologists explain resilience as the process of adapting well in the face of trauma, adversity, tragedy, threats, and stress. These include relationship and family problems, serious health issues, or stress from workplace and financial matters. Resilience involves "bouncing back" from these obstacles, and it can lead to profound personal growth. Jeffrey Gitomer describes resilience as how one reacts, responds, and recovers.

> *"Resilience is not what happens to you. It's how you react to, respond to, and recover from what happens to you."*
>
> —Jeffrey Gitomer

This chapter will discuss the importance of resilience in personal growth and the role of setbacks as opportunities for development. Moreover, it will shed light on the importance of fostering a growth mindset, practicing self-compassion, and creating a supportive environment for change.

FAILURE AND SETBACKS AS OPPORTUNITIES FOR GROWTH

> *"Do not judge me by my success; judge me by how many times I fell and got back up again."*
>
> —Nelson Mandela

Nelson Mandela's quote encapsulates embracing failure and repositioning it as an obstacle to growth. It emphasizes the value of resilience and the lessons learned from failure.

It would be best to shift your perspective to view failures as essential learning experiences. No one is perfect, and you must realize that setbacks will be inevitable. You must embrace those failures and reposition them as personal and professional growth obstacles.

An inspiring example of this mindset can be found in the story of Thomas Edison, the renowned inventor of the lightbulb. No one during those times knew that such an invention could take place, but with determination and the right mindset, he invented the first lightbulb.

In the 1920s, a journalist asked Thomas Edison how it felt to fail 1000 times when he tried to invent the lightbulb. To this, he replied,

> **"I didn't fail 1000 times. The lightbulb was an invention with 1000 steps."** [2]

Thomas Edison realized the potential for something and worked diligently to achieve it. With incredibly strong willpower to make his invention, his success was formed with habits, not just passion. We have discussed the formation of good habits and the breaking of bad ones in the first chapter. The idea is to understand that every misstep and stumble is only a step toward progress.

This is the mindset one needs to have when striving for a goal. This perspective highlights the importance of analyzing setbacks instead of getting demotivated and upset. You should extract lessons from them and identify areas for improvement.

---

2 https://medium.com/cry-mag/thomas-edisons-theorem-for-success-b96591bf7dd1

ANALYZE SETBACKS FOR IMPROVEMENT AND DEVELOPMENT

Analyzing setbacks is essential in identifying areas for improvement and development in your life. You need to realize that setbacks are a natural part of the journey toward growth. By understanding and taking a closer look at the challenges you face, you deeply understand yourself and uncover opportunities for personal growth. Following are a few ways on how you can go about it:

Embrace a Growth Mindset: Viewing setbacks as opportunities for learning and improvement rather than failures is a way of adopting a growth mindset. You must understand that setbacks do not define your worth or abilities but are stepping stones toward progress.

Reflect on the Setback: You should reflect on the setback you have experienced. Analyze the situation objectively and identify the factors that contributed to the setback. Was it a misunderstanding, lack of preparation, or external circumstances beyond your control? This kind of self-reflection will help you gain clarity.

Identify Patterns and Trends: Look for recurring themes or patterns in the setbacks you have faced. Are certain areas of your life or specific behaviors consistently leading to setbacks? Identifying these patterns can help you pinpoint areas where you need to improve.

Seek Feedback from Others: Don't hesitate to contact family members, mentors, or trusted friends for their perspective on the setback. They may offer alternative viewpoints or valuable insights that you hadn't considered. Their feedback can help you see things from different angles.

Set Specific Goals: Once you have identified areas for improvement, set specific goals to work on. Break them down into small steps. By setting clear objectives, you can stay motivated and measure your progress.

Learn from Mistakes: Focus on the lessons the obstacles provide and treat setbacks as opportunities for improvement and growth. Analyze the mistakes you made, learn from them, and use those lessons to make better choices and decisions in the future.

By analyzing setbacks and identifying areas for improvement, you take an active role in shaping your life. Learn from your experiences, remain committed to personal growth, and embrace the process of self-reflection. Think of every setback as an opportunity to become wiser, stronger, and more resilient.

EXPERIMENTATION AND RISK-TAKING TO PROMOTE GROWTH

Encouraging a culture of experimentation and risk-taking is crucial to promote growth. When you step outside your comfort zone and embrace new experiences, you open doors to untapped potential and personal development. Following are the ways to foster this culture within yourself:

Embrace the Unknown: Instead of fearing the unknown, cultivate a mindset that embraces it. It would be best if you were open to new ideas, challenges, and experiences that may initially seem uncertain or unfamiliar.

Emphasize Learning Over Perfection: Shift your focus from striving for perfection to valuing the process of growth and learning. Recognize that failures are part of the journey and give valuable lessons.

Encourage Curiosity and Exploration: Embracing curiosity helps you discover new paths for growth and fuels creativity. Seek out new experiences, ask questions, and actively explore diverse perspectives.

Embrace Calculated Risks: While taking risks can be scary, it's important to distinguish between calculated risks and reckless choices. Assess the consequences and potential benefits before embarking on a new venture. Evaluate the risks involved, plan accordingly, and be prepared to adapt and learn.

Emphasize Experimentation: Encourage yourself to experiment with different solutions and approaches. Please recognize that the first attempt may yield a different outcome than the desired outcome, but it is an opportunity to learn. You should embrace the concept of iteration, where you continually improve based on experience and feedback.

Surround Yourself with Supportive People: Seek out a supportive network of mentors, friends, or like-minded people who encourage experimentation and risk-taking. Surrounding yourself with people who share your mindset can guide and inspire your growth journey.

Celebrate Progress: Acknowledge and celebrate your progress, regardless of the outcome. Recognize that every step forward, regardless of failure or success, tests your patience and willingness to take risks.

You move toward personal growth and development by fostering a culture of experimentation and risk-taking. Embrace the unknown, learn from failures, and continually challenge yourself to expand your horizons. You must remember that growth often happens outside your comfort zone, and embracing this attitude will help you unlock your true potential.

ROLE OF FAILURE IN PERSONAL AND PROFESSIONAL DEVELOPMENT

Importance of Trial and Error in Skill Acquisition: In your journey toward personal and professional development, it is vital to recognize the importance of trial and error as an essential aspect of skill acquisition. As a young child learns to walk by taking uncountable stumbling steps, you should also embrace failure as a required part of your growth.

By approaching challenges with a curiosity and experimentation mindset, you allow yourself to refine your abilities and learn from your mistakes.

Acknowledge that Failure is Inevitable: In both personal and professional lives, it is essential to acknowledge that failure is an inevitable part of the journey to success. Just like Thomas Edison, many successful people have faced numerous setbacks and encountered failures along the way. Instead of viewing failure as an outcome, you must understand that it is just a stepping stone to success.

Thinking of failure as a natural part of the process, you can navigate challenges with perseverance and resilience.

Identify the Lessons from Past Failures: One of the most valuable aspects of failure lies in the lessons it provides.

When you face setbacks or experience failures, reflect on the circumstances and identify the lessons you can gain from them. Each failure holds wisdom and insights that can inform your future decision-making, allowing you to make better choices and avoid repeating past mistakes. By extracting the lessons from your failures, you understand yourself, your strengths, and areas for improvement.

Moreover, reflecting on past failures can help you assess what worked and what didn't, enabling you to refine your methods and develop more effective strategies moving forward. Learning from failure eventually leads to personal and professional growth, equipping you with the knowledge and skills necessary to succeed.

LEARN FROM MISTAKES AND USE THEM AS STEPPING STONES TO PROGRESS

Reflect on Past Errors: In your journey toward progress, it's vital to acknowledge that making mistakes is essential to learning and growth. It would be best to embrace them as valuable opportunities for self-improvement instead of dwelling on them. Take the time to reflect on your past mistakes and examine their root causes. This process will allow you to gain insights into your actions, decisions, and thought patterns that led to those mistakes.

During self-reflection, be honest with yourself. It's crucial to avoid self-judgment or blame. Instead, focus on understanding the factors contributing to the errors, such as the circumstances, external influences, your mindset, and the information available. By analyzing such root causes, you can identify reasons that may have hindered your progress in the past.

Implement Changes and Improvements Based on Lessons Learned: Once you have gained a deeper understanding of the root causes, use this knowledge to implement changes and improvements in your approach. Recognize that your mistakes were growth opportunities, and you can make more informed choices moving forward.

Create an actionable plan based on the lessons learned from your mistakes. Identify specific habits, behaviors, or strategies for improvement. This may help you avoid similar errors in the future.

Track Progress and Growth Over Time: As you implement changes and improvements, tracking your progress and growth over time is essential. This monitoring process is a source of motivation and helps maintain focus on your journey toward improvement.

Set measurable milestones that align with your goals and regularly evaluate your development. Document your achievements, no matter how small they may seem. Celebrate each milestone to learn from mistakes. This positive reinforcement will provide a sense of accomplishment and boost your confidence.

Moreover, you should periodically revisit your past mistakes and compare them with your current decisions and actions. This reflection will track your progress and help identify any remaining areas for improvement. Recognizing your growth will make you continue using mistakes as stepping stones toward further progress.

Remember, the journey of personal growth is an ongoing one. Embrace the lessons your mistakes teach you and view them as valuable opportunities to improve yourself. Implementing changes based on lessons learned, reflecting on past errors, and tracking your progress over time will transform mistakes into stepping stones for continuous improvement and achievement.

REFRAME SETBACKS AS VALUABLE FEEDBACK RATHER THAN PERSONAL DEFICIENCIES

When faced with setbacks, adopting a solution-oriented and constructive approach is essential. Instead of viewing them as personal deficiencies, view them as valuable feedback to help you improve. Embrace the mindset that challenges are opportunities for learning and development. Focus on identifying the underlying factors that contributed to the setback instead of dwelling on the negative aspects.

Doing so lets you develop action plans and strategies to move forward and overcome obstacles.

View Setbacks as Temporary and Isolated Incidents: Remember that setbacks are temporary and isolated incidents, not reflections of your self-worth. Everyone experiences ups and downs; it's a natural part of life's journey. It would be best if you refrained from attaching your value as a person to these setbacks. Instead, recognize that they are moments that provide valuable insights.

Moreover, think of them as learning experiences. This mindset allows you to detach emotionally from the setbacks, enabling you to analyze them accurately and make informed decisions on how to proceed.

Encourage Open and Honest Dialogue: It's important to encourage open and honest dialogue about failure to reframe setbacks as valuable feedback.

You should create a supportive environment where you can share your experiences openly without fear of judgment or ridicule. By discussing failures openly, you can gain different perspectives and insights, enhancing your ability to reframe setbacks and extract valuable lessons from them. Engaging in conversations about failure helps normalize setbacks and promotes problem-solving and collective learning.

GROWTH MINDSET THROUGH INCREMENTAL PROGRESS

In the book, "*Outliers: The Story of Success,*" Malcolm Gladwell repeatedly referred to the "10,000-hour rule," declaring that the key to achieving true expertise in any skill is to practice for at least 10,000 hours.[3]

Over time, when a person becomes skilled, it requires less time to accomplish the same task. However, it is significant to note that this rule only guarantees success. Instead, it serves as a guideline for the dedication and effort required to reach a high level of proficiency.

As people learn skills throughout their journey, they often experience a concept known as "skill acquisition efficiency." This means that as they become more skilled in a particular area, they can accomplish tasks more efficiently, requiring less time.

For example, a student enrolled in a course for his bachelor's program will have to study for around 15 to 20 hours per week. They will pursue mastery of the course through deliberate practice and regular feedback, leading to persistence and continuous learning.

In addition, people should celebrate small victories and milestones along the way to maintain motivation. This is one of the ways you can keep yourself motivated throughout the journey.

Rewarding and acknowledging yourself for each step forward, no matter how small, can help foster a positive mindset and prevent burnout. People can stay motivated and focused on their long-term goals by appreciating the progress made. Furthermore, people should recognize the cumulative effect of marginal gains on long-term success.

---

3 https://www.ncbi.nlm.nih.gov/pmc/articles/PMC4662388/#

"Small daily improvements are the key to staggering long-term results."

POWER OF SMALL, CONSISTENT IMPROVEMENTS

THEY SAY YOU NEED TO START WITH BABY STEPS IF YOU WANT TO achieve something big.

One way of achieving this would be creating positive habits through marginal changes to your habits that will make you successful gradually. Just as a single brick does not build a wall, minor changes and adjustments to your habits and behaviors may seem trivial in isolation, but their overall impact is significant.

Similarly, practicing a musical instrument for a few minutes daily or dedicating time for self-reflection and learning can seem insignificant. However, when viewed as a whole, they contribute to positive changes and transformations in your life.

CELEBRATE SMALL VICTORIES AND MILESTONES TO MAINTAIN MOTIVATION

While acknowledging the power of minor improvements, it's equally important to celebrate your small victories and milestones along the journey. Recognizing and appreciating these achievements is critical to stay on track and maintain motivation.

Take a moment to pause and reflect on how far you've come whenever you achieve a small goal or make progress toward your larger objectives.

Celebrate your accomplishments, no matter how trivial they may seem. Share your successes with others who can offer support and encouragement. By acknowledging and celebrating these small victories, you reinforce the positive changes that you have made.

IMPLEMENT DAILY ROUTINES AND HABITS

Consistency is vital when it comes to gaining the benefits of minor improvements. It's essential to implement daily routines and habits that promote steady progress. You should create a plan or set clear goals aligning with your long-term vision. Break down these goals into small, manageable tasks you can consistently work on. Incorporate these tasks into your daily routines.

Additionally, focus on the quality of your efforts rather than the quantity. Minor, consistent improvements require focus and dedication. You continuously improve your knowledge and skills by making incremental adjustments and learning from your experiences.

Remember, the path to success is often a series of small steps instead of a straight line.

By acknowledging the cumulative effect of marginal gains, celebrating your small victories, and implementing daily routines and habits that promote steady progress, you set yourself up for long-term success.

MINDSET FOCUSED ON EFFORT, LEARNING, AND ADAPTABILITY

To cultivate a mindset focused on effort, learning, and adaptability, it's vital to emphasize the value of dedication and hard work in achieving your goals. Understand that success hardly comes without perseverance and effort. You set yourself up for progress and growth by embracing a strong work ethic.

Recognize that failures and setbacks are part of the journey toward success. Instead of being discouraged by them, view them as opportunities to improve and learn.

Embrace the challenges, knowing each obstacle presents a chance to overcome limitations and develop new skills. By persisting through difficult times and remaining dedicated to your goals, you increase the possibility of achieving long-term success and building resilience.

ENCOURAGE CURIOSITY, EXPLORATION, AND CONTINUOUS SELF-IMPROVEMENT

A mindset focused on effort, learning, and adaptability thrives on curiosity, exploration, and continuous self-improvement. You should foster a sense of eagerness and wonder to explore new experiences, perspectives, and ideas. Embrace a growth mindset that believes in the potential for expansion and development.

Cultivate a love for learning by seeking out new skills and knowledge. Engage in lifelong learning through reading, attending workshops, taking courses, or pursuing hobbies that challenge you intellectually. Moreover, you should stay open-minded and be willing to step outside your comfort zone to welcome new growth opportunities.

DEVELOP PROBLEM-SOLVING AND CRITICAL-THINKING SKILLS

Developing strong problem-solving and critical-thinking skills is central to cultivating a mindset focused on effort, learning, and adaptability. These skills enable you to find innovative solutions, navigate challenges, and adapt to changing circumstances.

You should practice approaching problems with a solution-oriented mindset. Break down complex issues into small parts, analyze them objectively, and explore various perspectives. Cultivate your ability to think critically and evaluate information carefully.

Consider alternative approaches and seek out diverse viewpoints to expand your problem-solving toolkit.

Moreover, embrace a mindset of adaptability. Recognize that change is inevitable, and adaptability allows you to tackle uncertain situations. Embrace new trends, ideas, and technologies, and be willing to adjust your plans and strategies accordingly.

PERSEVERANCE AND PATIENCE IN ACHIEVING GOALS

Adversity is a natural part of any journey toward success. Instead of becoming disheartened by setbacks or obstacles, view them as opportunities for learning and growth. Embrace your challenges, for they are the stepping stones to success. Stay determined, maintain your focus, and remind yourself that achieving your goals may be challenging, but it is ultimately worth it.

PRACTICE DELAYED GRATIFICATION

In a world of instant gratification, practicing delayed gratification is a powerful skill essential for achieving long-term success. It requires resisting short-term temptations and staying committed to your goals, even when immediate rewards may not be apparent.

You should always maintain a long-term perspective on success. Understand that outstanding accomplishments take effort, time, and patience. You should keep your eye on the bigger picture and remind yourself of the ultimate goal you want to achieve.

DEVELOP COPING STRATEGIES AND RESILIENCE

The journey toward success is rarely a straight one. Setbacks and obstacles are inevitable along the way. Therefore, developing resilience and coping strategies is essential in maintaining motivation and overcoming challenges.

When faced with failures or setbacks, you should take the time to reflect and learn from the experience. It would be best to focus on solutions rather than the problems. Seek support from others who can provide encouragement and guidance during difficult times.

You should develop a toolkit of coping strategies that work for you. These may include practicing mindfulness, seeking inspiration from role models, engaging in physical exercise, or finding comfort in creative outlets. You can bounce back from setbacks and achieve success by cultivating resilience and adopting effective coping strategies.

CREATE A SUPPORTIVE ENVIRONMENT FOR CHANGE

As discussed in the first chapter, identifying the cues in your environment can contribute to incremental improvements.

Creating a supportive environment for change when striving for success and personal growth is critical. Let's consider the analogy of planting a seed to illustrate this notion. If a seed is planted in the soil, it will grow into a plant. However, if planted in rich soil and provided water, it will nourish into a beautiful and strong plant over time.

This example shows the importance of collaboration and networking in life. If you surround yourself with supportive people who root for you, you will eventually become successful. It is essential to connect with individuals who embody desired values and traits. You must establish a safe space for open communication, feedback, and encouragement. Moreover, establishing mentoring relationships with experienced individuals can provide valuable guidance and insights on your journey.

POSITIVE INFLUENCES AND ROLE MODELS

Regarding personal growth and development, surrounding yourself with role models and positive influences can be incredibly impactful. By identifying and connecting with people who embody desired values and traits, learning from their wisdom and experiences, and emulating their habits and positive behaviors, you can foster a supportive environment that leads to personal growth.

IDENTIFY AND CONNECT WITH INDIVIDUALS WHO EMBODY DESIRED TRAITS AND VALUES

To create a positive support system, it is essential to identify people who embody the traits and values you admire and aspire to. You should consider the following steps to help you in this process:

Reflect on Your Values: Take some time to identify the core traits and values you want to cultivate within yourself. This will serve as a guiding framework when seeking out role models.

Seek Like-Minded Communities: Join organizations, communities, or groups that align with your values and interests. Surrounding yourself with people who share similar values and goals can provide a fertile ground for finding positive influences and role models.

Engage in Networking: Attend conferences, events, and workshops related to your field of interest. Actively engage in conversations, ask questions, and seek connections with people who inspire you. Building a network of positive influences will be important in your growth journey.

Learn from the Experiences and Wisdom of Successful Role Models

Once you have identified positive influences and role models, making the most of their experiences and wisdom is essential. Following are some ways you can learn from them:

Establish Regular Communication: Reach out to your role models and express your appreciation for their achievements. Ask if they would be open to mentoring or offering guidance. Regular communication will allow you to benefit from their insights and learn directly from their experiences.

Ask Thought-Provoking Questions: Prepare a list of meaningful and thoughtful questions to help you understand their journey and how they overcame challenges. By asking the right questions, you can gain valuable insights.

Actively Listen and Observe: When engaging with your role models, observe their mindset, problem-solving skills, and decision-making process. Pay attention to their work ethic, communication style, and strategies for success and try to implement these into your life as well.

EMULATE POSITIVE BEHAVIORS AND HABITS TO FACILITATE PERSONAL GROWTH

It is crucial to emulate your role models' positive behaviors and habits to facilitate personal growth. Identify the specific habits and behaviors contributing to your role models' success. It could be their resilience, discipline, positive mindset, or adequate time management. Recognize these key behaviors and make a conscious effort to incorporate them into your own life. Your role models can serve as a source of inspiration and guidance throughout this process.

GUIDANCE AND MENTORSHIP FROM THOSE WHO HAVE OVERCOME SIMILAR CHALLENGES

When faced with challenges in your personal or professional life, seeking guidance and mentorship from people who have overcome similar obstacles can be invaluable. Establish mentoring relationships, participate in support groups and communities, and leverage a supportive network's collective wisdom and resources to receive the guidance and encouragement you need to deal with your challenges successfully.

ESTABLISH MENTORING RELATIONSHIPS WITH EXPERIENCED INDIVIDUALS

Mentorship is a powerful tool for personal growth and development.

Identify Potential Mentors: Look for people who have gone through similar experiences and achieved the goals you aspire to achieve. These mentors should have the knowledge and expertise to guide you effectively.

Reach Out and Express Your Intentions: Once you have identified potential mentors, reach out to them and express your admiration for their achievements. Clearly communicate your desire for mentorship and guidance, explaining how their experiences resonate with your challenges.

Foster a Mutually Beneficial Relationship: Establish a mentoring relationship that benefits both parties. Respect their expertise and time, and demonstrate your commitment to growth and learning. Actively seek their feedback, advice, and insights, and be open to constructive criticism.

PARTICIPATE IN SUPPORT GROUPS AND COMMUNITIES FOCUSED ON SHARED GOALS

Support groups and communities can provide a nurturing environment where you can meet people who have faced similar challenges. Consider the following steps to participate in these groups:

Research Relevant Groups and Communities: Look for support groups, online forums, or communities that focus on the goals or challenges you are currently facing. These groups often provide a safe space for seeking advice and sharing experiences.

Actively Engage and Contribute: Once you have joined a support group or community, actively engage by sharing your own experiences, insights, and challenges. Offer support and encouragement to others who are going through similar journeys. By actively contributing, you create an environment that fosters mutual support.

Seek Mentors within the Community: Within these groups, you may find people who have successfully overcome your challenges. Reach out to them and express your desire for mentorship and guidance. A mentor inside the community can provide you with valuable advice tailored to your specific circumstances.

LEVERAGE THE COLLECTIVE WISDOM AND RESOURCES OF A SUPPORTIVE NETWORK

Building a supportive network of people who have overcome similar challenges can provide you with a wealth of resources and wisdom. Here's how you can leverage this network effectively:

Expand Your Network: Actively seek opportunities to expand your network by attending workshops, conferences, and events related to your field or area of interest. Exchange ideas, engage in conversations, and build relationships with people who have faced similar challenges.

Share and Seek Knowledge: Share your experiences and insights within your network to contribute to the collective wisdom. Similarly, don't hesitate to seek other people's advice, opinions, and resources.

Maintain and Nurture Relationships: Regularly connect with your network, whether through virtual calls, in-person meetings, or online platforms. Building strong relationships within your network ensures continuous guidance and mentorship. Stay updated on each other's progress, celebrate successes, and provide support during setbacks.

ACTIVITIES AND ENVIRONMENTS THAT PROMOTE GROWTH AND RESILIENCE

To foster personal growth and resilience, it is essential to actively engage in activities and surround yourself with environments that promote these qualities. By pursuing hobbies that expand and challenge your abilities, attending conferences and workshops to gain new perspectives, and engaging in physical activities to enhance your emotional and mental well-being, you can create a supportive ecosystem for your personal development.

PURSUE HOBBIES AND INTERESTS THAT CHALLENGE AND EXPAND YOUR ABILITIES

Pursuing hobbies and interests that push your boundaries and expand your abilities can contribute significantly to your personal growth. You should consider the following steps to engage in these activities effectively:

Reflect on Your Passions and Interests: Take some time to reflect on the activities that genuinely inspire and excite you. Identify hobbies and interests that challenge you emotionally, intellectually, or creatively. These are the pursuits that have the potential to promote resilience and growth.

Set Goals and Seek Continuous Improvement: Set specific goals for your interests or hobbies. Break them down into smaller milestones and work toward achieving them. Embrace a growth mindset that emphasizes improvement and continuous learning.

Embrace Challenges and Embrace Failure: Don't be afraid to step outside your comfort zone. Remember that failures and setbacks are part of the learning process. Embrace them as opportunities for resilience-building and growth.

ATTEND WORKSHOPS, SEMINARS, AND CONFERENCES TO GAIN NEW PERSPECTIVES

Attending seminars, workshops, and conferences allows you to gain new insights, perspectives, and knowledge. Following are the ways to make the most of these opportunities:

Research Relevant Events: Look for seminars, workshops, and conferences related to your field of interest or personal growth goals. Explore diverse topics and select events offering valuable insights and practical takeaways.

Actively Participate and Network: Once you attend an event, ask questions, actively engage in discussions, and participate in group activities. Take advantage of networking opportunities to connect with like-minded people and experts in your field. Building connections can provide mentorship and ongoing support.

Apply Learnings to Real Life: Reflect on the insights and knowledge you gained after attending an event. Identify critical takeaways and consider how to apply them to your professional and personal life. Furthermore, experiment with new ideas and concepts, adapting them to your unique circumstances.

ENGAGE IN PHYSICAL ACTIVITIES AND EXERCISE TO ENHANCE MENTAL AND EMOTIONAL WELL-BEING

Engaging in exercise and physical activities has several benefits for emotional and mental well-being. Here are some tips for better well-being:

Choose Activities You Enjoy: Find physical activities that you genuinely enjoy. It could be dancing, running, yoga, hiking, or any exercise that brings you happiness.

Establish a Routine: Consistency is critical to reaping exercise's mental and emotional benefits. Incorporate physical activities into your daily or weekly routine. You should set realistic goals and gradually increase the intensity or duration of your activities over time.

Embrace Mindfulness: Use physical activities as an opportunity to practice mindfulness. Pay attention to your body, sensations, and the present moment. This can improve focus, help reduce stress, and enhance overall well-being.

SELF-COMPASSION AND MINDFULNESS

PRACTICING SELF-COMPASSION AND MINDFULNESS IS ANOTHER VITAL aspect of personal growth during times that require change. Developing self-awareness through self-reflection and introspection allows you to understand your emotions, thoughts, and behaviors more profoundly. It helps you to identify areas for improvement and make necessary changes.

However, it is essential to practice self-forgiveness and let go of self-criticism. During change, it is natural to make mistakes and face challenges. Treating yourself with empathy, kindness, and understanding during these difficult times is crucial. Recognizing that you are in the process of embracing growth and reinventing yourself allows you to navigate change with a positive attitude.

In line with self-compassion, adopting mindfulness practices can lead to personal growth. Mindfulness comprises being fully present in the current moment and observing your emotions and thoughts without judgment.

It allows you to cultivate a sense of focus, clarity, and resilience. By practicing mindfulness, you can make intentional decisions and better manage stress. It helps you to adapt to change more effectively and tap into your inner strengths. By nurturing these aspects, you can emerge stronger and navigate change gracefully, just like the bamboo that bends but remains resilient.

"The bamboo that bends is stronger than the oak that resists."

—Japanese Proverb

It is essential to build resilience during life's obstacles. Instead of perceiving your hardships as failures, you should reposition them as obstacles toward growth. Changing your perspective and realizing that every block or failure teaches you something can go a long way.

To create a supportive environment for change, you must surround yourself with supportive people and seek mentorship, establishing a safe space for open communication and collaboration. Moreover, practicing self-compassion, self-forgiveness, and mindfulness would be best, as they play a vital role in personal growth and resilience.

CHAPTER THREE

ACHIEVING GOALS

This chapter is about providing guidance on setting SMART goals, breaking them down into manageable steps, and tracking progress. The chapter will also highlight the importance of accountability, mentorship, motivation, and focus in achieving personal and professional goals.

SETTING SMART GOALS AND BREAKING THEM DOWN INTO SMALL STEPS

Everyone wants to achieve things in life. However, setting realistic goals will make it easier to achieve them. It's also going to be tough to measure how you are doing. The best approach is to break those big goals into chunks. That would combine short-, medium-, and long-term goals.

> *"A goal without a plan is just a wish."*
>
> —Antoine de Saint-Exupéry

Each has different benefits and can push you forward toward the desired result. Break down extensive or long-term goals into smaller weekly or daily ones to make them easier to focus on. Doing so will ensure that you're consistently taking steps toward achieving the life you desire, and it will also motivate you.

Following is a step-by-step goal-setting strategy to break down your goals and make them achievable:[4]

SET YOUR LONG-TERM GOALS FIRST

What do you want to achieve in the next few years? Ask yourself this question, and that's where you can start with your goal-setting strategy.

These long-term goals will take some time, like graduating from college, buying a home, or starting your own business. After all, such significant dreams require time and effort to achieve.

Before setting goals, it is crucial to identify your desired destination in the future. These long-term objectives serve as the foundation for your journey. Dreaming big with your goals is okay, but you need to be realistic about achieving them.

> *"Success is the sum of small efforts, repeated day in and day out."*
>
> —Robert Collier

Long-term goals should be achieved within a few years. Try to give your goals a time frame, such as buying a home in four years or completing writing a book in 30 days.

4 https://www.wendaful.com/2017/12/breaking-down-goals/

SET YOUR MEDIUM-TERM GOALS NEXT

Consider using these milestones as stepping stones to support your goal attainment. For instance, if purchasing a house is your ultimate objective, a medium-term goal could be saving 30% of the house deposit. This intermediary target is a reasonable milestone that bridges the gap between your current situation and the ultimate goal you aspire to accomplish.

Medium-term goals should also have specific time frames. These will keep you moving forward, ensuring you consistently work toward your aspirations and long-term goals.

FINALLY, FOCUS ON YOUR SHORT-TERM GOALS

These are goals that you can attain more readily. These will be actionable tasks that you can start right now. For example, set short-term goals for each quarter. You can start by setting a goal to research how much houses in your area cost, establish a way to create more passive income, a goal to decrease expenses, and a goal to meet with a realtor so that you can start planning for buying your new home. These goals will guide you toward your final goal.

You can set any short–term goals, but they should align with your big goals. This means they should be small but definite steps toward your desired goal.

Let's take an example. If you want to save up for a house, you must stop spending so much and allocate a certain amount of money into monthly savings.

Setting goals is essential. However, creating an action plan related to those goals is crucial in making them a reality. It is much easier to perform smaller chunks of work than to wing it toward whatever goal you aim for.

UNDERSTANDING THE SMART CRITERIA

Goals are part of every aspect of life and business. They provide a sense of direction, motivation, and a clear focus. By setting goals, you are providing yourself with a target.

A SMART goal is used to help guide goal setting. SMART is an acronym that stands for **Specific, Measurable, Achievable, Realistic,** and **Timely.**

Therefore, a SMART goal incorporates all of these criteria to increase the chances of achieving your goal.[5]

- *Specific: Well-defined, unambiguous, and clear.*

- *Measurable: With specific criteria that measure your progress toward the achievement of the goal.*

- *Achievable: Not impossible to achieve and attainable.*

- *Realistic: Realistic, within reach, and relevant to your life purpose.*

- *Timely: With a clearly defined timeline, including starting and end dates. The purpose of this is to create urgency.*

Sometimes, businesses or individuals will set themselves up for failure by setting general and unrealistic goals such as "I want to be the best at XYZ." The vagueness of this goal is a dead giveaway that it's unattainable. It has no sense of direction.

SMART goals set you up for success by making goals specific, measurable, achievable, realistic, and timely. The SMART approach will help push you further, give you a sense of direction, and help you organize and attain your goals.

5 https://corporatefinanceinstitute.com/resources/management/smart-goal/

TRACKING PROGRESS AND CELEBRATING MILESTONES

A GENERAL CONCEPT OF PROGRESS IS HOW GOOD IT FEELS TO achieve a long-term goal or major success. These big wins are great, but they are relatively rare. Thankfully, even small wins can increase self-satisfaction.

> ***"Remember to celebrate milestones as you prepare for the road ahead."***

This quote from Nelson Mandela should act as a reminder to take the time to reflect and celebrate even the small victories. Setting milestones and showing gratitude to your team can inspire them to reach their end goal.

Take the example of this diary entry from a programmer in a high-tech company, which showed positive self-ratings of her motivations, emotions, and perceptions that day.

"I figured out why something was not working correctly. I felt relieved and happy because this was a minor milestone."

When you are busy or working on mundane or tedious tasks, it can be challenging to take the time or even see your work for what it is – a small victory that brings us one step closer to the finishing goal. Yet, we must recognize the achievement.

Mehrnaz Bassiri, a Vancouver-based educator and public speaker, noted:

> *"Small wins have a transformational power. Once a small win has been accomplished, forces are set in motion to favor other small wins until the combination of these small wins leads to greater accomplishments."*[6]

---

6 https://www.niagarainstitute.com/blog/team-communication-tools

You can use methods such as journals, apps, or spreadsheets to monitor progress. You should explore different tracking tools to identify the most effective way for personal needs.

ESTABLISHING REWARDS AND INCENTIVES

A study conducted in 2018 compared the benefit of receiving frequent rewards for completing small tasks with the promise of a reward after finishing a long project. The researchers, Ayelet Fishbach and Kaitlin Woolley, found that participants experienced greater interest and enjoyment in their work when a small reward was available than those waiting for the delayed reward.[7]

At workplaces, highly engaged and motivated employees can be retained if the organizations can utilize incentives and rewards to recognize the contributions of employees and reward them for doing great work. People need to have specific incentives to motivate them to achieve their goals. Both internal and external factors can motivate a person to perform well.

Incentives and rewards motivate employees because they offer recognition of achievements and reward and reinforce positive behaviors. Incentives and employee recognition programs make employees more aware of their impact, give their work a greater sense of purpose, and motivate them to perform well consistently.

HOW INCENTIVES AND REWARDS BOOST MOTIVATION

Immediate rewards increase intrinsic motivation because they link goals and activities. Incentive programs can increase employee performance by up to 44% and motivate up to 66% of employees to stay with their organization. Companies that offer

7 https://nesslabs.com/self-motivation

tangible sales incentives see increases in annual revenue that are three times higher than those that don't offer incentives.[8]

Rewarding employees for their efforts and celebrating their achievements, hard work, and successes will let them know they are valued and that their work has an impact.

Incentives and rewards boost motivation because they reward the behaviors that underlie achievements and can improve values alignment. Incentives and rewards can help organizations improve engagement and retention and increase team morale and productivity.

POWER OF ACCOUNTABILITY AND MENTORSHIP

Arnold Schwarzenegger believes that the idea of a self-made man is a myth. During a session at the University of Houston, he said:

> *"I wouldn't be here without my parents, teachers, and mentors."*

If your friends and family know what you are trying to achieve, they will likely be more prepared and willing to help whenever possible. Finding a network of people who can guide and help you is essential for reaching your goals. Effective goal-setting requires you to share your goals with your network.

If the people in your life don't understand your goal or do not provide support to you, then you must look elsewhere.

Social media can be used to do this, as there are countless support networks online where people share ideas and thoughts. A quick search on Google will turn up various support networks and groups in major cities and areas worldwide.

---

8 https://businessleadershiptoday.com/incentives-and-rewards-for-motivating-employees/

> *"You are the average of the five people you spend the most time with."*
>
> —Jim Rohn

Spend time with people who are as accomplished as you or aspire to be. Surround yourself with like-minded people to grow your support network and be part of the networks of others.

You can start with your gym classes. Find those people in your classes or the events you attend who have similar goals and work to help each other succeed. Encourage people around you to push themselves and set increasingly challenging goals. Make an effort to extend support to others, as this act of kindness often reciprocates back to you. Additionally, consider seeking guidance from individuals with greater expertise and experience in your desired field. These mentors have achieved the level of success you aspire to reach.

Mentor-mentee relationships are invaluable as they can provide insights into the mistakes they have made during their journey, helping you avoid similar pitfalls. Failure is life's greatest teacher, but learning to avoid common pitfalls from someone who has been there before can save you valuable time and resources. Don't hesitate to reach out to someone you think fits the mold and can help and guide you.[9]

MAINTAINING MOTIVATION AND FOCUS

REFLECTING ON PERSONAL VALUES, PASSIONS, AND MOTIVATIONS

To begin setting goals that resonate with you, it is essential to dedicate some time to reflect on your values.

9 https://www.crossfitinvictus.com/blog/the-importance-of-social-support-in-achieving-your-goals/

Ask yourself: What aspects hold the utmost importance in my life? What do I want to represent or stand for? What are my priorities? By clearly understanding your values, you can use them as a compass while setting your goals, ensuring they are in harmony with what truly matters to you.

If your goals aren't aligned with your values, you will likely feel unfulfilled and disconnected, even after accomplishing them. When your goals align with your values, they become more inspiring and motivating, as they hold personal significance and bring fulfillment.

Let's take an example here. If you hold health as a core value, setting goals related to regular exercise and maintaining a healthy diet would be fitting.

Alternatively, if you prioritize spending time with your loved ones, you'd make time in your busy schedule to spend it with them. Utilizing your values as a guiding factor in aligning your goals is paramount. This approach ensures that you are actively progressing toward objectives that hold personal significance and remain consistent with your values. By incorporating your values into your goal-setting process, you can confidently pursue personally meaningful endeavors. You can follow a more rewarding and purpose-driven life by incorporating your values into your ambitions.[10]

IMPLEMENTING TIME MANAGEMENT TECHNIQUES

To achieve swift and effective results, mastering the skill of efficient time management is vital, both in your professional and personal endeavors. Fortunately, by strategically utilizing appropriate time management tools and techniques, you can signifi-

10 https://medium.com/@amisiga/aligning-your-values-with-your-goals-assures-inner-success-ef0729ce4448

cantly boost your productivity, efficiently structure your time, eliminate the occurrence of missed deadlines, and rapidly develop proficiency in time management.

The Pomodoro Technique is a notable example, as it assists in effective time management and cultivates favorable work habits. By successfully managing your time, you can accomplish more tasks within shorter intervals, derive a sense of fulfillment from your achievements, and mitigate the potential risks of burnout.[11]

CULTIVATING A GROWTH MINDSET AND A POSITIVE ATTITUDE

Replace negative beliefs, such as "I'm inadequate" or "I can't handle this," with positive ones, like "I can enhance my skills through practice" or "I am capable of learning this." This shift is crucial in developing a mindset that values growth and progress.

Believing that you can improve your abilities and intelligence through effort, learning, and feedback is known as having a growth mindset. Adopting a positive mindset allows you to perceive challenges as prospects for growth rather than threats or failures.

Furthermore, embracing mistakes and actively seeking constructive feedback is vital. Instead of avoiding or taking mistakes personally, they should be seen as valuable opportunities for learning and improvement. Challenges, in turn, become chances to acquire new knowledge and expand your capabilities rather than setbacks or obstacles.

Equally important is the willingness to explore uncharted territory and experiment with alternative approaches. Rather than sticking solely to what is comfortable or familiar, taking risks and trying new things promotes personal growth and fosters a mind-

11 https://www.timedoctor.com/blog/time-management-tools-and-techniques/

set of continuous learning and adaptation. Finally, it is essential to celebrate your efforts and progress. Never compare yourself to others because everyone's journey is different.[12]

RECOGNIZING THE VALUE OF PERSEVERANCE AND RESILIENCE DURING ADVERSITY

How often have you faced a challenge in life and given up on it or yourself the first time without having the courage and strength to learn, grow, and learn from your experiences or mistakes? How has that decision affected you while moving forward?

We all face obstacles in life, and resilience is about overcoming them, stepping up to the challenges, and dealing with the practical and emotional consequences of negative experiences. You should also be able to move on from them better, stronger, and wiser.

Resilience is all about the mindset and thought process to maintain focus and overcome challenges, and perseverance is only giving up once you get there.

It's like Dory says in Finding Nemo, *'Just keep swimming, just keep swimming.'* Perseverance is critical when faced with initial setbacks; persistence is the driving force behind eventual success. However, putting these positive habits into action requires considerable effort. It includes developing self-control, taking responsibility for our actions, and fostering self-motivation. These characteristics are crucial in forming our character and developing our leadership abilities. Ultimately, we must be the leaders we desire and take command of our own lives, as relying on others to play this role is improbable. We give ourselves the power to forge our

12 https://www.linkedin.com/advice/0/how-do-you-cultivate-growth-mindset-embrace-challenges

pathways and design the future we want by embracing self-discipline, taking ownership, and creating self-motivation.

CONCLUSION

RATHER THAN SETTING UNREALISTIC GOALS, EMPLOYING THE SMART goal-setting framework can significantly increase your chances of success.

Breaking down long-term goals into smaller, manageable ones helps maintain focus and progress tracking. Celebrating milestones along the way serves as positive reinforcement and boosts motivation. Effective time management techniques and tools are crucial in achieving your goals.

Furthermore, having a supportive network and seeking guidance from mentors are essential to your journey toward success.

PART 2

RELATIONSHIPS

CHAPTER FOUR

COMMUNICATION

This chapter focuses on the importance of effective communication in building and maintaining relationships. It will also include active listening, empathy, clear self-expression, conflict resolution, and understanding nonverbal communication.

UNDERSTANDING THE IMPORTANCE OF ACTIVE LISTENING

Active listening is a soft skill that shifts the focus from what's in your head to the words coming from the outside world. By focusing on what another person is saying, you can understand information and needs more accurately.

Active listening requires the following:

- *Summarization*
- *Not interrupting*
- *Repeating what you hear back*
- *Picking up on body language*

STRATEGIES FOR ACTIVE LISTENING

Stop:

Please focus on the other person, their feelings, and thoughts. You must give your full attention to the speaker.

Listen:

Listen for the essence of the speaker's thoughts: details, major ideas, and their meanings. You should seek an overall understanding of what the speaker is trying to communicate rather than reacting to the person's words that they use to express themselves.

Be Empathetic:

Try to imagine how you would feel in their circumstances. You should be empathetic to the feelings of the speaker while remaining calm yourself. You need not be drawn into all of their problems or issues as long as you acknowledge what they are experiencing.[13]

13 https://uwaterloo.ca/centre-for-teaching-excellence/catalogs/tip-sheets/effective-communication-barriers-and-strategies

"You can't truly listen to anyone and do anything else simultaneously."

—M. Scott Peck

WHY ACTIVE LISTENS MATTERS FOR YOUR SUCCESS?

Being an engaged listener is essential for success in both school and business. This is because learning requires attention to the big picture and minute details. When you actively listen, your employer can see the difference between the work that follows and your responses.

In the interview stage during the recruitment process, active listening plays a significant role. By paying close attention and making eye contact with the interviewer, you can prove that you are interested in the position, can help with problem-solving, and can work well in a team.

In communication, listening is often disregarded. Most people are so focused on speaking and sharing their own experiences that they may need to remember that listening is a skill that requires constant attention and practice.

Let's take an example of this case to explain it in a better way. When you introduce yourself to a new person, you probably have experienced asking them their name. Then, while they tell you their name, you are thinking about saying it next. You haven't listened to their name, and you're embarrassed to ask again.

This is the issue so many people face in communication. Our minds can easily wander into our heads and imagine what's coming next or fall back into the past. That's why active listening is crucial. It's the only way to stay truly present in communication.

To stay truly present in our current situation, most people must practice this as both a skill and a reminder. Most people get caught up in passive listening instead of active listening. Passive learning means that they aren't listening. While they may not be interrupting, they are not asking questions or not providing feedback to understand the speaker.[14]

DEVELOPING EMPATHY

> *"Empathy is like a universal solvent. Any problem immersed in empathy becomes soluble."*
>
> *—Simon Baron-Cohen, British clinical psychologist and professor of Developmental Psychopathology, University of Cambridge*

Gaining a deep understanding of others' emotions is significant as it facilitates conflict resolution and enhances interpersonal relationships.

Surprisingly, although many individuals feel self-assured in acquiring new technical skills, they often need help to hone their interpersonal abilities. Furthermore, discussing one's own emotions can evoke self-consciousness in many individuals.

Empathy is the ability to recognize other's emotions and understand other people's perspectives on a situation. It helps you to use that insight to improve someone else's mood and to support them through challenging situations.

Empathy is often confused with sympathy, but they are not the same. Sympathy is a feeling of concern for someone. However, empathy involves sharing emotions or perspectives. It is putting yourself in another's shoes. It would be best to use open-ended questions to promote deeper conversation and uncover underlying emotions. Your excellent verbal communication skills will help you succeed in your professional and personal life.

---

14 https://www.uopeople.edu/blog/why-is-active-listening-important/

FIRMING UP VERBAL COMMUNICATION SKILLS

Verbal communication refers to the use of language to convey information. Verbal communication skills represent more than speaking abilities. They demonstrate how you deliver and receive messages in written and spoken interactions. These skills focus on how you communicate rather than what you say. Because of this, you can utilize nonverbal techniques like body language to improve your interactions.

Examples of practical verbal communication skills include:

- *Active listening*
- *Recognizing and responding to nonverbal cues*
- *Asking for clarification*
- *Asking open-ended questions*
- *Using humor to engage audiences*
- *Speaking clearly and concisely.*

Verbal communication skills matter because they enable you to build rapport with others, creating stronger work relationships and more positive interactions. With these skills, you can convey a sense of confidence and ensure that your audience understands your message or expectations. The ability to communicate helps you succeed in various work situations, including negotiations, job interviews, and projects.

PRACTICING VULNERABILITY AND HONESTY

> *"Vulnerability is about having the courage to show up and be seen."*
>
> —Brene Brown

When we resist vulnerability, we hear a "voice" telling us we shouldn't be open. Still, we're denying the people close to us by not allowing them to know us fully. We fear rejection or hurt, but vulnerability draws people in. We're doing ourselves and the other person a favor by being open. Many of us struggle with vulnerability because of fear, but we also fail to ultimately realize all of the ways we distance ourselves from others. It may feel like we're doing the right thing by keeping our mouths shut when we should actually be doing the opposite.

Our willingness to be vulnerable and tolerate intimacy matters in terms of relationships. A few years ago, researcher Brene Brown conducted thousands of interviews and concluded that vulnerability is essential in building connections.

> *"There can be no physical intimacy, emotional intimacy, spiritual intimacy—without vulnerability."*
>
> —Brene Brown

One of the reasons there is such an intimacy deficit today is that we don't know how to be vulnerable. It's about being honest with how we feel, what we need, and our fears. All in all, vulnerability is the glue that holds intimate relationships together.[15]

ROLE OF EFFECTIVE COMMUNICATION IN RESOLVING CONFLICTS

> *"The single biggest problem in communication is the illusion that it has taken place."*
>
> —George Bernard Shaw

Conflict occurs when there is a clash between people due to different thoughts and interests. To avoid or resolve conflicts, one needs to learn how to adjust to others.

This is when communication comes in. It has been observed time and again that most conflicts are a result of ineffective com-

15 https://www.psychalive.org/embracing-vulnerability-strengthens-connections/

munication. In reality, ineffective communication leads to most of the conflicts and misunderstandings.

Conversely, establishing and maintaining effective communication channels enables individuals to comprehend better one another's perspectives, thoughts, and needs. By fostering this open exchange of information, it becomes easier to understand others' viewpoints and approach specific situations collaboratively. Ultimately, improved understanding through effective communication facilitates productive teamwork and enables the collective pursuit of optimal solutions.[16]

NONVERBAL COMMUNICATION AND BODY LANGUAGE

Non-verbal communication is as important as verbal communication. There are many different types of non-verbal communication. They include:

- *Body movements (kinesics) such as nodding and shaking the head.*
- *Posture, such as how you stand or sit, whether your arms are crossed.*
- *Eye contact refers to the amount of eye contact that often determines the level of trust.*
- *Para-language aspects of the voice apart from speech, such as tone, pitch, and speaking speed.*
- *Closeness or personal space (proxemics) determines the level of intimacy and varies very much by culture.*
- *Facial expressions, which include frowning, smiling, and blinking. Interestingly, the broad facial expressions that show strong emotions, such as anger, fear, and happiness, are the same throughout the world.*

16 https://franticallyspeaking.com/11-effective-communication-strategies-to-resolve-conflict/#:~:text=There%20are%20many%20communication%20strategies,your%20relationship%20with%20the%20person.

- *Physiological changes mean that you may sweat or blink more when you are nervous, and your heart rate is also likely to increase. These are almost impossible to control consciously and determine a person's mental state.*

CONCLUSION

Both verbal and non-verbal communication skills hold significant importance in effective communication. Additionally, practicing empathy toward those around you is crucial.

You can better comprehend someone else's experiences and feelings if you put yourself in their situation. Furthermore, being human requires accepting vulnerability and being open with others. Recognizing and accepting this critical aspect of our humanity fosters meaningful connections and promotes genuine interactions. Also, being an active listener can help you during conflict resolution.

CHAPTER FIVE

STRENGTHENING BONDS

Cultivating robust and positive connections, personal or professional, is fundamental for our overall happiness and well-being. These relationships act as support pillars, providing love, empathy, and encouragement.

Fostering healthy bonds with partners and family brings immense joy and fulfillment within our circles. By investing time and dedication into these relationships, we create enduring connections that can withstand challenges and hardships.

To build healthy relationships, essential elements include open communication, trust, and empathy. Actively listening to our loved ones, understanding their emotions, and being a reliable presence in their lives is crucial.

Similarly, on a professional level, nurturing strong relationships is paramount. Positive interactions with colleagues, supervisors, and team members create a conducive work environment that enhances productivity and job satisfaction. Building a network of supportive colleagues and mentors can offer valuable insights and opportunities for growth. Collaborative and respectful relationships at the workplace lead to better teamwork and problem-solving, contributing to the success of projects and the overall organization.

Maintaining healthy and strong relationships is an investment in our well-being and success. It requires active effort, understanding, and effective communication. By prioritizing the connections we share with others in personal and professional realms, we create a sense of belonging, support, and fulfillment that enriches our journey through life. Now, let's discuss some practices and strategies that will help us strengthen our bonds and rekindle the severed relationships.

CULTIVATING GRATITUDE AND APPRECIATION

Cultivating gratitude and appreciation is fundamental in maintaining and strengthening any relationship. Expressing gratitude is a simple yet profound way to show love and recognition to the significant people in our lives. It acknowledges the efforts, kindness, and support our loved ones provide, making them feel valued and cherished. Cultivating gratitude and appreciation is a crucial aspect of fostering healthy relationships.

However, in today's society, self-centeredness and narcissism can often obstruct this process. Many prioritize their needs, inadvertently overlooking the importance of others around them. This self-centered behavior challenges forming and sustaining meaningful connections with friends and acquaintances.

To counteract the negative impact of self-centeredness, we must strongly emphasize nurturing gratitude and appreciation within our relationships. It is not uncommon to encounter individuals who prioritize their own needs and desires, overlooking the value of others in their lives. Making and maintaining genuine ties with friends and acquaintances is made difficult by this self-centered conduct.

We must strongly emphasize fostering thankfulness and appreciation within our relationships to combat the detrimental effects of self-centeredness. People who put their personal needs and wants above the importance of others are common to come across. Making and keeping meaningful ties with friends and acquaintances is made difficult by this self-centered conduct.

Reminding ourselves to be thankful for the friendships in our lives is the first step. Friends offer invaluable support, understanding, and shared experiences. Expressing gratitude for their time, efforts, and contributions demonstrates our sincere regard for their presence, nurturing deeper connections and mutual respect.

> *"When you stop expecting people to be perfect, you can like them for who they are."*
>
> —Donald Miller

It is essential to understand that no friend, just like no person, is perfect; everyone has flaws. Every person has particular talents and shortcomings. By accepting this fact, we can focus on the good things about our connections and set reasonable expectations. We can take specific attributes from our friends and value them for the unique aspects they offer to our lives, much to how we approach love partners.

Family ties are frequently predetermined, but friendships give you the freedom to choose. We can choose companions based on shared beliefs, pastimes, and experiences. This flexibility allows us to create a close-knit group of friends who enhance our lives and benefit our well-being.

Cultivating gratitude and appreciation in friendships benefits us individually and strengthens our social connections' bonds. When friends feel genuinely valued and appreciated, they are more likely to reciprocate these feelings, fostering a harmonious and fulfilling relationship.

EMBRACING OPEN-MINDEDNESS AND MINDFULNESS

Maintaining healthy and strong relationships necessitates adopting an open mindset and a willingness to find common ground, even when disagreement arises. This approach involves approaching conversations with empathy and understanding, valuing diverse perspectives and opinions to foster mutual respect and deeper connections.

Incorporating mindfulness into this mindset is essential, especially in today's fast-paced and technology-driven world, where genuine presence during social interactions is often lacking. The prevalence of smartphones and distractions can hinder authentic engagement in conversations.

Consider a scenario where friends gather, but each person remains engrossed in their devices, occasionally contributing to the conversation. This behavior inhibits meaningful connections as people miss fully engaging in the moment.

This challenge tends to be more pronounced among the younger generation, highlighting the significance of mindfulness for all age groups to strengthen relationships. Mindfulness entails non-judgmental awareness of thoughts, feelings, and surroundings, facilitating deep connections. By setting aside distractions and engaging in conversations, we demonstrate respect and create an environment conducive to genuine interactions.

At its core, this mindset underscores the value of gratitude and expressing appreciation for others. Being mindful and present allows us to genuinely recognize and acknowledge the efforts and contributions of those around us. By expressing heartfelt gratitude for their presence and impact on our lives, we reinforce the positive aspects of our relationships.

Fostering a mindful and open mindset and practicing gratitude and appreciation is a powerful means of strengthening relationships. Embracing diverse perspectives and being fully present during interactions builds trust and understanding. Let us strive to cultivate mindfulness, relinquish distractions, and convey genuine appreciation for the people who enrich our lives, forging deeper, more profound connections that endure over time.

> *"Silent gratitude isn't much use to anyone."*
>
> —Gertrude Stein

To incorporate gratitude into our relationships, we can start by regularly expressing our thanks. We all might silently appreciate and feel grateful for others in our hearts, but they will never know what we think if we never say it out loud. A heartfelt "thank you" for the little things goes a long way in creating a positive atmosphere. We should be specific in our appreciation, highlighting the actions or qualities we admire in the other person. This shows that we pay attention to and cherish the unique aspects that make them special.

Acts of kindness and thoughtful gestures can also strengthen our connections. Surprise your partner, family member, or colleague with small tokens of appreciation, like a handwritten note, a favorite treat, or a kind compliment. These actions demonstrate that we care and are willing to invest effort in making them feel loved and valued.

Moreover, active listening is a crucial component of expressing gratitude. When someone shares their thoughts or feelings with us, we should be fully present and attentive, showing empathy and understanding. This validates their experiences and fosters a deeper emotional connection.

Practicing gratitude can help defuse tension and foster forgiveness in times of conflict or challenges. Acknowledging the positive aspects of the relationship and the efforts made by both parties to resolve issues can pave the way for reconciliation.

Consistency is critical to maintaining gratitude as a core practice. Regularly remind ourselves to be grateful for the people we care about, even during busy or stressful times. By making gratitude a habit, we reinforce the positive aspects of the relationship, making it resilient to challenges.

Cultivating gratitude and appreciation is a vital aspect of building strong and lasting connections with our loved ones, both personally and professionally. The simple act of expressing gratitude can transform ordinary moments into cherished memories.

It is an ongoing practice that requires effort and intention, but the rewards are immeasurable, fostering a more profound sense of love, trust, and support within our relationships.[17]

POWER OF QUALITY TIME AND SHARED EXPERIENCES

> *"Spending time with those you love is the foundation of any strong relationship."*
>
> —Joseph Simmons

17 https://www.psychologytoday.com/us/blog/comfort-gratitude/202006/why-expressing-gratitude-strengthens-our-relationships

Spending quality time and sharing experiences is a cornerstone of building and strengthening relationships. Whether with family, friends, or colleagues, these shared moments create bonds beyond superficial interactions. Dedicating time to meaningful connections cannot be emphasized enough, as it lays the groundwork for trust, understanding, and emotional closeness.

Investing quality time with our loved ones demonstrates that we cherish and value them, as we are fully present in their company. By setting aside distractions and giving undivided attention, we communicate that they are a priority in our lives. Engaging in heartfelt conversations and shared activities during these moments allows for deeper connections, nurturing empathy, and forging cherished memories that last a lifetime.

Shared experiences play a vital role in bonding with others. Engaging in activities together, whether exploring new places, pursuing shared hobbies, or overcoming challenges, strengthens the sense of camaraderie and teamwork. These experiences build a reservoir of shared memories, laughter, and joy, further solidifying individuals' emotional connection.

Spending quality time together provides opportunities for effective communication. In these moments of undivided attention, we can express our thoughts, feelings, and vulnerabilities more openly. This honest communication cultivates trust and allows for the resolution of conflicts, leading to healthier and more harmonious relationships.

BUILDING STRONG RELATIONSHIPS IN A MILLENNIAL WORLD

In today's fast-paced world, quality time and shared experiences in fostering meaningful connections cannot be overstated, especially for millennials prioritizing experiences over material possessions. For many, creating shared memories through activities holds greater importance than acquiring things. Engaging in experiences together forges powerful bonds and deepens connections between people.

This philosophy isn't limited to personal relationships; it also extends to the corporate realm. Progressive companies recognize the impact of shared experiences on team building and employee engagement. They organize events outside the workplace and after-hours gatherings to encourage employees to connect on a more personal level. These shared experiences offer several advantages in building a positive work culture and boosting team dynamics.

One of the critical benefits of shared experiences is their ability to create emotional connections among participants. Whether facing challenges together or enjoying leisure activities, these experiences evoke shared emotions and foster camaraderie. These emotional connections increase trust, empathy, and mutual support among team members, which is essential to a thriving work environment.

Shared experiences provide unique opportunities for meaningful conversations that might not happen in the regular workplace. Individuals tend to be more relaxed and open to discussing personal experiences, aspirations, and challenges outside their routine tasks. These deeper conversations enhance understanding and strengthen bonds between colleagues.

Being mindful and present during these shared experiences is crucial. When fully engaged, participants can genuinely appreciate the significance of the moment and the connections being formed. Mindfulness allows individuals to focus on the present, immerse themselves in the activity, and be receptive to the thoughts and feelings of others.

To fully harness the power of shared experiences, prioritization is critical. Whether in personal or professional settings, making time for these activities demonstrates a commitment to the relationships and their significance. Setting aside time for shared experiences conveys that these connections are valued and cherished.

The importance of quality time and shared experiences resonates with individuals of all ages. Engaging in activities builds emotional connections, fosters meaningful conversations, and strengthens relationships.

Organizing events and offsite activities in the corporate world enhances team dynamics and creates a positive work culture. By being mindful, present, and prioritizing these shared experiences, we cultivate deeper connections and create lasting memories with those we care about, enriching our lives and the lives of others.

IMPORTANCE OF BALANCING WORK AND RELATIONSHIPS

> *"In pursuing professional success, never nurture the personal bonds that truly enrich your life."*
>
> —Tony Robbins

Workaholics often face a common challenge in this competitive age – prioritizing professional commitments over personal relationships. Inadvertently, they may find their connections languishing due to this neglect. To foster deep, meaningful, and emotional relationships, dedicating quality time and genuine presence to our loved ones is vital.

Active listening plays a pivotal role in nurturing strong connections. Being fully engaged in conversations, giving undivided attention, and genuinely absorbing the thoughts and emotions of others shows that we value and respect their perspectives. This strengthens the bonds of understanding and empathy, fostering more profound connections.

Engaging in activities and unique experiences further enhances the connection among individuals. Shared experiences create lasting memories and strengthen the emotional bond. Engaging in new hobbies, embarking on adventures, or simply enjoying leisure time together all enrich relationships and foster a strong sense of togetherness.

> *"Life is a delicate dance between work and relationships; find the rhythm that brings you joy and fulfillment."*
>
> —Robin Sharma

Balancing personal and professional commitments is a continual challenge, and striving for a perfect equilibrium at all times may not be feasible, as life's demands can vary and shift our focus between different aspects. Flexibility is essential in recognizing shifting priorities and making intentional choices to nurture personal and professional relationships.

Workaholics and individuals facing demanding schedules must be mindful of the impact of neglecting personal relationships. By dedicating quality time, actively listening, and engaging in shared experiences, they can strengthen their connections with others. Achieving a perfect balance may not always be possible, but acknowledging the need for adjustment and prioritization is crucial. Balancing personal and professional commitments requires flexibility and understanding, leading to a more fulfilling life with strong, thriving relationships.

Spending quality time and sharing experiences with others is paramount for building and strengthening relationships. It showcases our commitment, fosters trust, and nurtures emotional connections. These shared moments create lasting memories and form the fabric of meaningful relationships in both personal and professional spheres. Let us prioritize quality time with our loved ones and colleagues, as through these shared experiences, we forge bonds that can withstand the test of time.[18]

NURTURING GROWTH IN RELATIONSHIPS

Supporting the growth and development of our loved ones is more than just being understanding and empathetic. It means actively participating in their journey toward personal fulfillment and success. Providing constructive feedback and encouragement creates a supportive environment that fosters accountability and helps them stay committed to their goals and dreams. Celebrating their achievements, no matter how small, becomes a way to acknowledge their progress and maintain motivation along the path to success.

As supportive friends or partners, we show our genuine care by engaging in active listening, dedicating meaningful time, and offering unwavering emotional support whenever they need it. We go beyond mere encouragement by empowering them to chase their aspirations, providing valuable guidance, mentorship, and access to resources that help them overcome challenges and reach their long-term objectives. By actively participating in their growth and development, we strengthen our connections and unveil the genuine essence of meaningful relationships.

The concept of celebrating achievements along the way is essential in this process. People often focus solely on the final destination, overlooking the significance of the journey and the progress made during the process. Whether completing a college course, advancing in a career, or achieving milestones in personal projects, celebrating small victories fosters a sense of accom-

18 https://cupla.app/blog/how-quality-time-can-transform-your-relationship/

plishment, boosts morale, and motivates you to keep pushing forward.

This principle extends beyond personal relationships; it applies to professional settings. Leaders and colleagues can support each other in the workplace by acknowledging and celebrating progress toward shared objectives. Recognizing efforts and milestones creates a positive work environment, enhances team morale, and inspires dedication to achieving collective goals.

Altogether, supporting the growth and development of our loved ones is an enriching journey that involves understanding, encouragement, empowerment, and celebration. By actively participating in their aspirations and achievements, we strengthen the bonds that connect us and create a nurturing environment for personal and collective growth. Remember that small, incremental steps make the most significant impact, and by appreciating the progress along the way, we can ensure lasting motivation and fulfillment in our relationships and endeavors.

ESTABLISHING HEALTHY BOUNDARIES IN SUPPORTING GROWTH

> *"Support and criticism are most impactful when delivered within the confines of healthy boundaries, for they become the foundation for growth and respect."*
>
> —John Smith

BEING SUPPORTIVE AND ENCOURAGING IS GOOD, BUT ALWAYS REmember to be within limits and never cross the boundaries. Establishing healthy boundaries is a crucial aspect of supporting the growth and development of our loved ones. While encouragement, feedback, and communication play essential roles in nurturing relationships, it's important to strike a balance and be mindful of limitations. Sometimes, individuals may unknowingly cross the line between constructive feedback and overwhelming pressure, leading to potential harm rather than motivation.

Recognizing and respecting personal boundaries is essential for fostering a healthy and nurturing environment. Each person has their comfort levels and sensitivities regarding communication and support. Being aware of these boundaries allows us to tailor our approach accordingly, ensuring that our words and actions are encouraging and helpful rather than discouraging or intrusive.

Moreover, it's essential to communicate openly and honestly about boundaries. Whether seeking motivation or providing support, both parties involved should express their needs and expectations clearly. This open dialogue fosters an environment of trust and respect, preventing misunderstandings and ensuring that the relationship remains positive and supportive.

Setting boundaries does not mean withholding support or neglecting to offer guidance. On the contrary, it means understanding and respecting the other person's space and emotional limits. It involves being sensitive to their feelings and acknowledging when they need space or time to process things independently.

Establishing healthy boundaries creates a safe space for growth and development. It allows individuals to feel secure in seeking help or feedback without fear of being overwhelmed or judged. This sense of safety and respect contributes to a deeper trust and openness within the relationship.

So, recognizing and respecting healthy boundaries is a crucial aspect of supporting the growth and development of our loved ones. It involves understanding the fine line between encouragement and pressure, sensitivity to individual comfort levels, and openly communicating about needs and expectations. By doing so, we foster an environment of mutual respect and trust, ensuring that our support and motivation genuinely contribute to the well-being and progress of our loved ones.

IMPORTANCE OF CONTINUOUSLY REASSESSING AND UPDATING BOUNDARIES

Continuously reassessing and updating boundaries is crucial to maintaining healthy and evolving relationships. As personal growth and life circumstances change, so do our relationship needs and expectations. A dynamic process, reassuring and adapting boundaries, allows individuals to grow together while respecting each other's individuality and autonomy.

In romantic relationships, a new connection's initial excitement and intensity may evolve into a deeper, more profound bond. As the "new relationship energy" settles, couples can establish a more stable and enduring foundation. Regular and open communication becomes essential during this phase. Honest conversations about desires, goals, and personal growth help partners understand each other's evolving needs and ensure their boundaries align with changing circumstances.

In any relationship, whether personal or otherwise, ongoing communication is critical to understanding and respecting each other's boundaries. As individuals grow and evolve, their boundaries may shift, and what was once acceptable might no longer be comfortable. Individuals can navigate potential conflicts and challenges by engaging in open dialogue and actively listening to each other's concerns and desires with compassion and assertiveness.

Respecting the boundaries of others requires empathy and understanding. Acknowledging that different people have different comfort levels and needs helps foster a culture of acceptance and support within relationships. It involves being attentive to cues and being adaptive in our behavior, ensuring that our actions align with what is acceptable and comfortable for the other person.

Navigating conflicts and difficult conversations with compassion and assertiveness ensures that healthy boundaries are maintained. When disagreements arise, it's crucial to approach them with empathy and a desire to understand the other person's perspective. Balancing compassion with assertiveness allows individuals to assert their needs while also being considerate of the feelings and needs of others.

Building and maintaining strong relationships require continuous reassessment and adaptation of boundaries. By regularly reassuring and updating these boundaries, individuals can create a safe and supportive space for personal growth and mutual understanding. Practicing empathy, active listening, and open communication are essential elements in respecting each other's boundaries. Navigating conflicts with compassion and assertiveness further strengthens the bonds within relationships, fostering an environment of trust, respect, and growth for everyone involved.

CONCLUSION

THIS CHAPTER HAS HIGHLIGHTED THE PROFOUND IMPORTANCE OF supporting the growth and development of our loved ones as a powerful means of strengthening relationships and bonds. By understanding their aspirations, offering constructive feedback, and encouraging them, we create a nurturing environment that fosters trust, empathy, and mutual respect. Celebrating their achievements is equally vital, as it acknowledges their progress and maintains motivation for continued growth.

However, it is crucial to establish healthy boundaries in our support, ensuring that it remains empowering and never intrusive. Continuously reassessing and updating these boundaries as individuals evolve promotes enduring and fulfilling relationships.

With active listening, open communication, and compassion, we build a foundation of understanding and mutual support, laying the groundwork for lasting connections and meaningful companionships. Embracing these principles, we embark on a journey of shared growth and discovery, weaving stronger bonds that withstand time and enriching our lives with love, encouragement, and shared aspirations.

By prioritizing the growth of our loved ones and being present in their journey, we create a harmonious environment where personal and collective development thrives. This chapter serves as a reminder that nurturing relationships through support and celebration is a continuous and rewarding process, enriching our lives with genuine connections and lasting joy. As we cherish each other's dreams and accomplishments, we build a future of shared growth and fulfillment together.

PART 3

CAREER AND PROFESSIONAL DEVELOPMENT

CHAPTER SIX

DEVELOPING SKILLS

Skills development is not merely a choice but an inherent aspect of human progress. Reflecting on personal growth, one can undoubtedly observe their transformative journey. Comparing the present self to the past reveals a host of differences, showcasing the power of skill development in enhancing efficiency and capabilities. Taking a moment to introspect and jotting down these disparities on paper allows for a deeper understanding of one's journey and the significance of honing specific tasks and abilities.

The human brain is a remarkable organ, continually evolving and learning from the challenges it encounters. Each obstacle presented an opportunity to acquire new skills, proving that our minds can adapt and develop specific capabilities with focused training and instructions.

So, why is skills development essential? The answer lies in parallel with teaching a child to communicate or walk on two feet. These fundamental teachings are vital for survival, ensuring better and more efficient adaptation to life's demands. Equipping individuals with essential tools for survival and prosperity, skill development plays a pivotal role in human nature.

It fosters personal growth and efficiency, empowering individuals to thrive in a constantly evolving world. By continuously learning and acquiring new abilities, people gain the capacity to navigate life's challenges effectively, resulting in enhanced proficiency and a greater sense of success and fulfillment.[19]

Developing one's skills begins with setting clear and achievable targets. It involves engaging in a simple self-assessment to identify both strengths and weaknesses. This reflective process lays the foundation for a structured and focused approach to skill development.

Setting targets is like charting a roadmap to success. By defining specific goals, individuals understand what they want to achieve and the skills they need to acquire. These targets act as guiding beacons, keeping individuals motivated and committed to their growth journey.

Skill development is deeply connected to our personal and professional objectives and goals. Once we have established these aspirations, we can build a solid foundation for skill enhancement by aligning our efforts with our desired outcomes.

On a personal level, setting objectives helps us identify the areas of self-improvement we wish to pursue. Whether learning

19 https://elearningindustry.com/skills-development-how-to-develop-your-skills

a new language, developing creative talents, or improving time management, having clear personal goals provides direction and purpose to our skill development journey. These goals may enrich our personal lives and contribute to overall well-being and fulfillment.

Similarly, in the professional realm, setting career objectives allows us to identify the skills required to advance and excel in our chosen fields. Whether it's becoming proficient in particular software, honing leadership abilities, or improving communication skills, knowing our professional goals helps us prioritize skill development efforts. These targeted improvements benefit our careers, enhance our value to employers, and contribute to overall professional growth.

IDENTIFYING WEAKNESSES AND STRENGTHS THROUGH SELF-ASSESSMENT

"Knowing yourself is the beginning of all wisdom."

—Aristotle

SELF-ASSESSMENT PLAYS A CRUCIAL ROLE IN THE PROCESS OF SKILL development. When we are required to analyze our strengths and weaknesses candidly, it entails honest introspection to recognize areas of strength and expertise, acknowledging the skills that can be leveraged for further improvement. Simultaneously, identifying weaknesses allows individuals to pinpoint the areas that require development, providing direction for focused learning efforts. Understanding our weaknesses will enable us to identify skill gaps that must be addressed.

This self-awareness is vital in devising a tailored plan for skill development, ensuring that we focus on areas that require improvement and capitalize on our existing strengths. Let's take a look at the steps involved in the process of self-assessment:

Reflect on Past Experiences: Reviewing past accomplishments and challenges can offer insights into areas where we excel and areas needing improvement.

Seek Feedback: Asking for feedback from colleagues, mentors, or friends can provide an outside perspective on our strengths and areas for growth.

Analyze Performance: Evaluating our performance in various tasks or projects can help identify patterns of strengths and weaknesses.

Take Personality and Skill Assessments: Utilize personality or skill assessments to understand your traits and abilities better.

Journaling: Keeping a journal of achievements, challenges, and personal observations can help recognize recurring patterns and areas for improvement.

Conduct SWOT Analysis: Perform a personal SWOT analysis (Strengths, Weaknesses, Opportunities, and Threats) to identify internal strengths and weaknesses and external opportunities and challenges.

Set Goals: Establish clear objectives and goals for personal and professional development, which will naturally reveal areas where additional skills are needed.[20]

By regularly engaging in self-assessment and cultivating a positive and growth-oriented mindset, we can better understand ourselves, continuously improve, and maximize our potential for success in various aspects of life.

---

20 https://www.wikihow.com/Identify-Your-Strengths-and-Weaknesses

CULTIVATING A GROWTH MINDSET FOR COMPREHENSIVE PERSONAL DEVELOPMENT

> *"The view you adopt for yourself profoundly affects how you lead your life."*
>
> —Carol S. Dweck

As we progress in our skill development journey, adopting a growth mindset is essential. Embracing the belief that our abilities can be developed through dedication and hard work encourages us to overcome challenges and persist in our efforts. This mindset shift fosters resilience and adaptability, enabling us to face obstacles with a positive attitude and a willingness to learn from setbacks.

Let's break down the components of a growth mindset to make it easier to understand and adapt.

Belief in Potential: A growth mindset is founded on the belief that our abilities and intelligence can be developed through dedication and hard work. We recognize that effort and perseverance are essential for growth and improvement.

Embracing Challenges: Individuals with a growth mindset embrace challenges as opportunities for learning and growth. They see difficulties as stepping stones to progress rather than obstacles that define their capabilities.

Persistence and Resilience: A growth mindset involves staying resilient despite setbacks. Instead of giving up, individuals with this mindset view failures as learning experiences, using them to adapt and improve.

Effort as the Path to Mastery: A growth mindset emphasizes the value of action and continuous learning. It recognizes that mastery comes from consistent practice and the willingness to push beyond one's comfort zone.

Learning from Feedback: People with a growth mindset are open to feedback and constructive criticism. They see feedback as valuable input for improvement and use it to enhance their skills and knowledge.

Inspiration from Others: Individuals with a growth mindset find inspiration in the success of others. Rather than feeling threatened, they see successful individuals as role models and sources of motivation to strive for their achievements.

Viewing Setbacks as Temporary: A growth mindset helps individuals view setbacks as temporary and solvable. They do not interpret challenges as indications of their fixed abilities but as opportunities for growth and development.

Emphasizing the Process: Instead of solely focusing on results, a growth mindset emphasizes the process and the journey of learning and improvement.

Seeing Learning as Rewarding: People with a growth mindset find fulfillment in the learning process. They enjoy acquiring new knowledge and skills, regardless of external rewards.

Accepting and Learning from Mistakes: A growth mindset involves taking mistakes as part of the learning process. Instead of being discouraged, individuals see mistakes as chances to understand areas that need improvement.

By nurturing these components, individuals can cultivate a growth mindset that empowers them to approach challenges with optimism, embrace continuous learning, and achieve tremendous success and fulfillment in their pursuits.[21]

---

21 https://www.lifehack.org/357234/5-ways-cultivate-growth-mindset-for-self-improvement

BALANCING STRENGTHS AND WEAKNESSES

Embracing our strengths and weaknesses is essential for comprehensive personal development. Many individuals tend to play to their strengths and overlook flaws, but a growth mindset encourages a different approach. By recognizing and accepting our strengths and weaknesses, we can adopt a more balanced and practical approach to skill development.

One way to address weaknesses is by actively working to strengthen them. Identifying areas that need improvement allows us to create targeted plans for growth. By dedicating time and effort to developing these weaker areas, we enhance our overall skill set and become more well-rounded. This approach fosters adaptability, as we are better equipped to handle various tasks and challenges.

On the other hand, building upon our strengths can also be a viable strategy. Leveraging our strong points allows us to excel in specific areas, becoming experts or specialists in those fields. Focusing on our strengths can lead to higher confidence and expertise, setting us apart and opening up new opportunities.

Self-reflection plays a crucial role in this process. Taking time to assess our abilities and identifying areas of strength and weakness provides valuable insights. By honestly acknowledging these aspects, we can create a personalized roadmap for growth, optimizing our personal development journey.

Assessment tools and feedback from mentors are invaluable resources for self-improvement. Personality tests, skill assessments, and performance evaluations provide objective insights into our strengths and areas needing development. Seeking guidance from mentors or trusted individuals allows us to gain external perspectives and valuable advice, enhancing our self-awareness and growth trajectory.

Moreover, a growth-oriented mindset encourages us to view weaknesses as opportunities rather than limitations. We recognize that continuous learning and development are integral to personal growth, and we embrace challenges as stepping stones to progress. This positive outlook fuels our motivation to strive for improvement and empowers us to embrace change and adapt to new circumstances.

ANALYZING SKILL GAPS FOR COMPREHENSIVE DEVELOPMENT

In creating a comprehensive development plan, analyzing skill gaps becomes crucial to maximizing our potential as candidates. Let's say that when reviewing a job description, it is essential to identify the specific skills and qualifications required and compare them to our existing skill set. This analysis helps determine where we may fall short and need improvement.

The first step is to assess which skills from the job description we possess. These are our strengths, and we should highlight them in our application to showcase our suitability for the role. Next, we identify the skills we need to improve or have partially developed. We need to address these skill gaps to become a more competitive candidate.

After identifying the skill gaps, the next step is to evaluate whether other strengths we possess can offset the missing skills. For instance, if the job requires strong technical expertise but lacks a particular technical skill, we can highlight our problem-solving abilities or adaptability as compensating strengths that may still make us a valuable asset to the company.

Creating a comprehensive development plan involves setting clear objectives to enhance the skills we lack. We prioritize the skill gaps based on their importance to the job and our career goals. For instance, if a specific skill is critical for our desired role, it becomes a top priority for improvement. Other skills may be categorized as secondary, which we can work on once we address the primary skill gaps.

The plan may include various learning methods, such as enrolling in courses, attending workshops, seeking mentorship, or gaining hands-on experience through projects or internships. Additionally, we can leverage online resources, educational platforms, and networking opportunities to enhance our skills.

It's essential to track our progress regularly and reassess our development plan. As we acquire new skills, we should update our resume and emphasize the newly acquired abilities in our job applications. A growth-oriented mindset allows us to embrace challenges and remain committed to continuous improvement, setting us apart as proactive and determined candidates in the job market.

Analyzing skill gaps when considering job opportunities is vital to creating a comprehensive development plan. By identifying our strengths and addressing the areas where we need more expertise, we can enhance our employability and become more competitive candidates. Prioritizing skill development and a growth mindset empowers us to present ourselves as well-rounded and capable professionals, ready to thrive in our chosen careers.

Skill development thrives on the foundation of objectives and goals that we set for ourselves, both personally and professionally. We can identify skill gaps and chart a personalized growth path by assessing our strengths and weaknesses. A growth mindset further amplifies our potential, allowing us to continuously evolve and thrive in our pursuit of skill enhancement, leading to a more fulfilling and successful life journey.

With targets set and self-assessment completed, individuals can design a personalized plan for skill development. After discussing the power of mindset and assessment, the next question that comes to mind is how we will make those improvements.

SMART GOALS: A PATHWAY TO COMPREHENSIVE PERSONAL DEVELOPMENT

A POSITIVE AND GROWTH-ORIENTED MINDSET LAYS THE FOUNDATION for improvement and growth. Once we embrace the concept of continuous development, the subsequent step involves devising a comprehensive development plan aligned with our objectives and aspirations. This plan includes setting short-term and long-term goals to enhance our skill set and achieve overall personal growth.

Goals are pivotal in propelling progress and maintaining focus on our development journey. Regardless of their scale, goals offer clarity and purpose. Long-term objectives define our ultimate destination, while short-term goals act as stepping stones toward reaching them.

To ensure practical goal setting, the SMART framework offers a valuable tool. SMART is an acronym representing Specific, Measurable, Achievable, Realistic, and Timely. Adhering to these criteria enhances our focus and significantly increases the likelihood of achieving our goals.

By embracing the SMART framework, we empower ourselves to set well-structured goals that are specific, measurable, achievable, realistic, and timely. This systematic approach maximizes our chances of success and supports our personal and professional growth journey. These goals provide clarity, focus, and motivation, empowering us to navigate our journeys with purpose and intention. They act as a roadmap, guiding our actions, tracking progress, and allowing for necessary adjustments.[22]

A well-rounded development plan necessitates a balance between short-term and long-term objectives. Short-term goals provide immediate targets, motivating us with achievable accomplishments. They generate momentum as we witness incremental progress. Long-term goals maintain focus on the bigger picture, offering direction and purpose.

Dividing our goals into manageable milestones and tasks aids in effective achievement. This process mitigates feeling overwhelmed and enables steady, achievable strides toward our objectives. Every achieved milestone becomes a building block on our path to growth, propelling us toward our long-term vision.

Regularly reviewing and adjusting our development plan is vital for adequate progress. Periodic reassessment enhances adaptability and allows course corrections when needed. Celebrating achievements, no matter how small, reinforces motivation and commitment to continuous improvement.

Goal-setting is an influential means to accomplish improvement and personal growth. By amalgamating short-term and long-term objectives, employing the SMART framework, and segmenting goals into manageable milestones, we can create a comprehensive development plan that balances aspiration with feasibility. Embracing a growth mindset and consistently striving for gradual improvement, we progress on our self-development journey, unlocking our full potential and attaining more significant success in all aspects of life.

22 https://www.mygreatlearning.com/blog/smart-goals/

UNLOCKING POTENTIAL THROUGH CONTINUOUS SELF-IMPROVEMENT

"Once you stop learning, you start dying."

—Albert Einstein

LIFELONG LEARNING AND THE POWER OF CURIOSITY ARE INTERtwined forces that propel personal growth and success. Lifelong learning entails pursuing knowledge and skills continuously, extending beyond formal education. It underscores the notion that learning extends throughout life, embracing an ongoing voyage of exploration and advancement.

The potency of curiosity lies in its capacity to ignite fascination and stimulate exploration. Curiosity drives us to pose questions, seek answers, and delve deeper into captivating subjects. It is the driving force behind learning and the gateway to uncovering fresh insights and comprehension.

Embracing a growth mindset, nurturing curiosity, and engaging in various learning methods all create a positive attitude that propels us toward continuous growth and lifelong learning. We open ourselves to the potential for boundless improvement and development by challenging our barriers and beliefs.

Cultivating a positive attitude is the foundation of this transformative journey. It involves reframing challenges as opportunities and failures as stepping stones to success. With a positive outlook, we approach learning enthusiastically, embracing the joy of acquiring new knowledge and skills. This optimistic mindset empowers us to face obstacles with resilience and determination, continually striving for improvement.

As we nurture our curiosity, we become more curious and open to exploration. Curiosity drives us to seek diverse learning experiences and consider new perspectives. It ignites a hunger for knowledge that knows no bounds, leading us to delve into various subjects and fields of interest.

Engaging in different learning methods, such as reading, taking courses, or attending workshops, enriches our learning journey. It allows us to access a vast pool of knowledge and expertise, providing diverse sources of information and learning opportunities. Lifelong learning becomes a continuous pursuit, transcending the boundaries of traditional education.

Combining a growth mindset, curiosity, and various learning methods creates a self-reinforcing cycle of continuous improvement. As we learn, our confidence grows, motivating us to embrace new challenges and explore uncharted territories. Each learning experience fuels our desire for more knowledge, fostering a lifelong love for learning and personal development.

With a positive attitude, we challenge our barriers and beliefs, recognizing that they are not fixed limitations but opportunities for growth. This attitude shifts our perspective from a fear of failure to a curiosity for learning. We understand that there is always room for improvement and that each experience, whether positive or challenging, presents valuable lessons for personal growth.

Learning for life involves a dedication to continuous improvement, encompassing both significant and minor aspects. It goes beyond mastering a single skill and becoming complacent; instead, it entails constantly honing and expanding our skill sets. We actively pursue opportunities for enhancement, even in the simplest tasks, to broaden our abilities and embrace new experiences.

Identifying our skill set is a crucial step in this journey. Understanding our strengths and weaknesses allows us to create targeted development plans, focusing on areas that require improvement while leveraging existing talents. As we improve our skills, we gain confidence in our abilities and embrace a proactive approach to growth.

Never stop learning becomes more than a catchphrase; it becomes a way of life. This mindset empowers us to be agile, adaptable, and relevant in an ever-changing world. As we cultivate a thirst for knowledge, we understand that the journey of learning has no end, and every stage of life presents growth opportunities.

Embracing a learning-for-life approach is a powerful mindset prioritizing continuous self-improvement and growth. It entails recognizing that learning is a lifelong journey beyond formal education. By consistently seeking opportunities to enhance ourselves and refining even the most minor aspects of our abilities, we unlock our full potential and experience a fulfilling and purposeful life.

UNLOCKING POTENTIAL THROUGH NETWORKING AND MENTORSHIP

"Your network is your net worth."

—Porter Gale

NETWORKING AND MENTORSHIP ARE INVALUABLE PILLARS OF PERsonal and professional development, as powerful tools to expand opportunities and enhance individual capabilities. Embracing a learning-for-life approach, these practices empower individuals to build meaningful connections, seek guidance from experienced mentors, and open doors to valuable insights and growth opportunities.

Individuals create a supportive community that promotes continuous growth and learning by fostering connections with like-minded peers and industry experts. In this dynamic landscape of self-improvement, networking, and mentorship are essential ingredients for unlocking one's full potential and achieving success in various aspects of life.

Networking and mentorship are powerful tools for expanding opportunities and enhancing individual capabilities. By building connections with like-minded individuals and experts, we open doors to valuable insights, guidance, and growth opportunities.

Building Connections: Networking enables us to connect with people in our industry or fields of interest. Industry conferences, events, workshops, social groups, and online forums are great platforms to meet like-minded individuals and experts. These connections can lead to valuable collaborations, learning opportunities, and professional growth.

Seeking Mentorship: Mentorship is a valuable relationship that provides guidance and support from experienced individuals. Mentors don't necessarily have to be older; they can be younger or of the same age but possess unique experiences and expertise relevant to our desired skills and goals.

Learning from Experience: Engaging in mentorship allows us to learn from the experiences and insights of others. Mentorship accelerates our learning process by providing valuable advice and knowledge that might take years to acquire independently.

Mutually Beneficial: Mentorship is a two-way street. Mentors provide guidance and wisdom, while mentees bring fresh perspectives, new ideas, and specific skills or assistance to the relationship. Mutual respect and a shared eagerness to learn from one another are essential foundations for this dynamic partnership.

Online Learning: Besides mentorship, online courses, and learning platforms offer accessible and flexible avenues for gaining new skills and knowledge. These platforms provide various courses in various subjects, empowering us to enhance our capabilities on our terms.

Continuous Growth: Networking and mentorship contribute to constant growth and development. By surrounding ourselves with knowledgeable and experienced individuals, we create an environment conducive to learning and improvement.

Confidence and Support: Mentorship provides a support system that boosts confidence and motivation. Knowing we have someone knowledgeable to turn to for guidance can help us tackle challenges more resilient and determined.

Expanding Opportunities: Networking expands our professional network, increasing the chances of discovering new opportunities, collaborations, and potential career advancements.

Creating a Supportive Community: Engaging in networking and mentorship helps us become part of a supportive community. It connects us with individuals with similar goals and aspirations, fostering a sense of belonging and camaraderie.

Networking and mentorship play crucial roles in personal and professional growth. By building connections with like-minded individuals and experts, we create opportunities for learning, collaboration, and career advancement. Engaging in mentorship allows us to gain insights from experienced individuals, accelerating our growth and expanding our capabilities.

Online learning complements these experiences, providing accessible and flexible ways to acquire new skills and knowledge. Embracing networking and mentorship creates a supportive environment for continuous improvement, enabling us to thrive and achieve our goals in various aspects of life.

EMBRACING CONSTRUCTIVE CRITICISM AND VALUING FEEDBACK FOR GROWTH

IN OUR GROWTH JOURNEY, SURROUNDING OURSELVES WITH like-minded individuals and seeking mentorship makes feedback integral to the process. However, it's essential to acknowledge that feedback isn't always supportive or positive; it can also come as criticism. Maintaining a balanced mindset empowers us to leverage feedback effectively, using it to advance professionally and personally.

When we engage with like-minded people and seek mentorship, we expose ourselves to diverse perspectives and insights, resulting in feedback that can be encouraging or challenging. Positive feedback boosts our confidence and validates our efforts, while criticism compels us to examine our weaknesses and areas for improvement.

To embrace feedback constructively, understanding its role in our development is crucial. Feedback is a valuable information source, providing self-awareness and uncovering blind spots. Approaching feedback with an open mind and curiosity, rather than defensiveness, allows us to appreciate its significance.

Appreciating the insights offered by experienced individuals is vital to leveraging feedback constructively. Mentors can offer guidance we might have yet to consider otherwise, shedding light on new strategies and pushing us to think critically, fostering growth beyond our current capabilities.

When facing criticism, asking ourselves how the feedback helps us is vital. This question guides us in evaluating the feedback's relevance and applicability to our objectives. Rather than viewing criticism as a personal attack, we can see it as an opportunity for improvement and self-reflection.

Balancing feedback involves distinguishing the intent from the delivery. The message may be valid, even if the delivery could be better. Focusing on the core message allows us to extract valuable insights and apply them to our growth journey.

Feedback is also a tool for developing self-awareness. By examining our reactions to feedback, we gain insights into our emotional responses and thought patterns, addressing areas for growth in managing feedback effectively.[23]

The example of professional athletes like Tom Brady, who invest in personal coaches alongside their team coaches, illustrates the value of seeking personalized feedback and guidance. While team coaches focus on improving performance within the team context, personal coaches can provide individualized support, optimizing all aspects of an athlete's life.

Tom Brady's investment in a personal coach and chef highlights his commitment to maximizing his potential. While not everyone has the resources to invest millions in personal coaching, the key takeaway is the mindset: the understanding that feedback, guidance, and continuous improvement are crucial for achieving excellence in any field.

> *"Feedback is the key to improvement."*
>
> —Bill Gates

Valuing the feedback we receive is fundamental to growth. Constructive criticism offers valuable insights that challenge us to confront our weaknesses and identify areas for improvement. By

---

23 https://www.linkedin.com/advice/1/how-do-you-deal-feedback-criticism-from-growth

embracing constructive criticism, we foster a receptive mindset that positions us for growth and advancement.

Continuing communication with those providing feedback ensures ongoing support and learning. Engaging in open and transparent conversations helps us gain a deeper understanding of the feedback's context and allows us to ask clarifying questions. By actively seeking feedback and staying open to it, we demonstrate our commitment to personal growth and development.

> *"To grow, one must be willing to embrace feedback and learn from it."*
>
> —John C. Maxwell

Recognizing the value of feedback is essential, even when it is not immediately apparent. Sometimes, feedback may be uncomfortable or challenging, but it can be an opportunity for self-reflection and refinement. Viewing feedback as a gift and a chance to enhance our skills empowers us to make positive changes and move closer to our goals.

When we encounter feedback that we question or find difficult to assimilate, seeking input from peers, supervisors, and friends can provide additional perspectives. These objective viewpoints can help us gain clarity and identify areas where improvement is needed.

Similarly, in personal relationships, seeking objective viewpoints from a third party can effectively gain clarity and resolve issues.

Couples facing challenges often benefit from an unbiased perspective that helps them understand their needs and goals and solve their problems. Creating a feedback loop of criticism and positive reinforcement fosters open communication and constructive discussions. Building upon this feedback and embracing a receptive mindset enables them to develop an improvement plan, promoting growth and strengthening their relationship.

Ultimately, developing a growth-oriented mindset and valuing feedback are foundational personal and professional development principles. The example of successful athletes like Tom Brady reminds us that embracing feedback, seeking guidance, and investing in continuous improvement are key elements in reaching our full potential.

CONCLUSION

This chapter covered the transformative journey of personal and professional growth. It started by emphasizing the importance of identifying areas for improvement and setting targets to achieve our objectives. Lifelong learning and the power of curiosity are celebrated as the driving forces that fuel continuous development and adaptability in an ever-changing world.

Then came the highlights of the significance of networking and mentorship as catalysts for growth. By building connections with like-minded individuals and seeking guidance from experienced mentors, we open ourselves to invaluable insights and opportunities.

Furthermore, the chapter explored the art of embracing feedback and constructive criticism. It emphasized the value of maintaining a receptive mindset, appreciating the role of feedback in our growth journey, and using it as a tool for continuous improvement.

As we integrate these principles, we see personal and professional growth as an ongoing process where each interaction, experience, and feedback loop contribute to our evolution. By embracing challenges, seeking objective viewpoints, and nurturing a thirst for knowledge, we empower ourselves to thrive, learn, and never stop evolving.

At last, it unveiled the power of a growth-oriented mindset. By combining targeted goals, curiosity-driven learning, meaningful connections, and constructive feedback, we create a recipe for continuous growth and success. As we move forward with a commitment to lifelong learning and self-improvement, we embark on a fulfilling journey toward achieving our highest potential and positively impacting our lives and the world around us.

CHAPTER SEVEN

LEADERSHIP AND INFLUENCE

When we hear the word "leader," we often visualize a forceful, charismatic figure like a historical icon or a military commander. However, leadership is not an adjective; it doesn't require extroverted charisma. Charisma doesn't automatically equate to effective leadership.

Leadership transcends seniority or hierarchical positions within a company. Often, people mistakenly equate a company's leadership with its top executives, but they are senior officials. A specific salary level does not automatically confer authentic leadership; while one might hope to find it there, it's not guaranteed.

Titles do not define leadership. Just because you hold a high-ranking title, like the one at the C-level, doesn't inherently make you a "leader." I emphasize that leadership can exist without a title. You can be a leader in your community, family, or religious setting, even without a formal designation.

Leadership and management are distinct. The most crucial distinction is that leadership and management are not interchangeable. Having a team of 15 people under your supervision and being responsible for profit and loss is commendable in a managerial capacity. Effective leadership involves planning, measuring, coordinating, solving, hiring, firing, and dealing with operational aspects. Managers typically oversee tasks, while leaders guide people.

Becoming a leader unveils a fundamental truth sooner or later—actions hold more weight than mere words. While you can preach tirelessly about the significance of hard work, dedication, and honesty, your words lose their impact if you don't practice what you preach. This is precisely where leading by example becomes pivotal, proving that actions carry more weight than empty rhetoric.

As a leader, it's imperative to recognize that your actions will serve as a source of inspiration, for better or worse, and that every move you make will undergo close examination. As Kim Scott eloquently put it in "Radical Candor," being a leader is akin to being scrutinized following an arrest; *everything you say or do can be used against you.*

By exemplifying the behavior you wish to see, you convey to others that you're willing to back up your words with actions.

Let's delve into leading by example and elucidate its importance in effective leadership. What exactly does leading by example entail?

Leading by example constitutes a leadership approach wherein you set a precedent through your actions, conduct, and attitudes. It encompasses showcasing the qualities and behaviors you anticipate from others and embodying the actions you aspire to witness in your surroundings.

When wielded skillfully by capable leaders, it becomes a potent instrument capable of inspiring and motivating others to attain remarkable outcomes. However, it necessitates a sense of greatness from you as well.

Consider an everyday scenario. Envision yourself outdoors with your grandmother, who's imparting the skill of riding a bicycle. Rather than merely instructing you to get on the bike and pedal, she demonstrates equilibrium on the bike, pedaling techniques, and proper brake usage. She supports the back of the bike and runs alongside you, cheering and encouraging you as you struggle to maintain balance. This is leading by example.

She doesn't merely offer verbal guidance; she backs it up with her actions. As she leads through her example, your confidence and belief in your abilities begin to burgeon. Witnessing her pedaling beside you, you think, "If she can do it, so can I." Before long, you're pedaling independently while your grandmother remains by your side, motivating you. She has illustrated the way; now it's your moment to shine.

Likewise, team leaders who lead by example don't confine themselves to verbal instructions; they exhibit the "how" through their actions, setting a precedent for others to follow. Like parents, leaders must embody the conduct they desire to observe in others.

EXEMPLARY LEADERSHIP: INSPIRING THROUGH ACTIONS

"Leading through demonstration" pertains to showcasing desirable behaviors, traits, and actions to exert influence and inspire others to emulate. It encompasses establishing a benchmark through your behavior and decisions, motivating others to adopt similar conduct for personal development, growth, or enhancing a collective, institution, or community.

Here are a handful of everyday instances illustrating leading through demonstration:

HEALTH AND WELLNESS

When you uphold a regular fitness routine, prioritize nutritious eating habits, and manage stress effectively, your lifestyle can inspire friends, family, or colleagues to give precedence to their well-being. Your unwavering commitment to a healthy lifestyle acts as a blueprint that motivates others to adopt comparable routines.

WORK PRINCIPLES

By showcasing punctuality, unwavering dedication, and a robust work ethic in your professional role, you can ignite the aspiration within coworkers to elevate their performance. Consistently meeting deadlines and delivering top-tier work can catalyze colleagues to amplify their productivity and contribute positively to the team.

COMPASSION AND EMPATHY

Practicing kindness, empathy, and inclusiveness in your interactions can have a ripple effect, compelling those around you to treat others with compassion and respect. When you actively listen, extend a helping hand, and factor in others' emotions, you set the stage for an environment where individuals are inspired to do the same.

SUSTAINABLE PRACTICES

Initiating measures to reduce your carbon footprint, recycle, and conserve resources can prompt friends and family to embrace more eco-conscious habits. Your eco-friendly choices establish a precedent for others to follow, adding to collective endeavors to safeguard the environment.

COMMUNITY ENGAGEMENT AND VOLUNTEERING

By partaking in volunteer initiatives and engaging with your local community, you help others channel their time and energy into worthwhile causes. Your involvement can act as an impetus for individuals to take an active role in addressing societal concerns and effecting positive change.

LIFELONG LEARNING

An eagerness for knowledge and a steadfast commitment to self-improvement can stimulate others to pursue continuous learning. Sharing insights derived from reading, participating in workshops, or acquiring new skills can inspire a culture of constant advancement.

DISPUTE RESOLUTION

Managing conflicts constructively and courteously can serve as a model for others to resolve disagreements peacefully. Your approach to addressing differences can cultivate a harmonious atmosphere and fuel open peer communication.

Leading through demonstration involves personifying the behaviors and principles you desire to witness in others. Using unwavering actions and discerning choices, you kindle the aspiration in individuals to mirror positive attributes, cultivating an environment characterized by development, cooperation, and affirmative transformation.

CULTIVATING EXEMPLARY LEADERSHIP

In leadership, forging a path of influence goes beyond merely guiding with words. Authentic leadership is a transformative journey that involves embodying qualities, embracing growth, and setting an inspirational example. This journey is encapsulated by the ethos of leading by example. It's about stepping into uncharted territories, leveraging feedback, and embodying resilience and adaptability.

As leaders strive to foster growth within themselves and their teams, they embrace the wisdom of reinvention, recognizing that it's not just about facing challenges but about evolving in the process.

PROACTIVE PURSUIT OF GROWTH

Embracing the philosophy of leading by example involves a proactive pursuit of personal development and skill enhancement. This transformative journey is marked by an insatiable thirst for new insights and an unwavering embrace of constructive feedback. These twin tools serve as the catalysts propelling your relentless quest for progress and self-improvement.

VENTURING INTO THE UNFAMILIAR

At the heart of this voyage is an unflinching readiness to venture into uncharted territories. Recognizing that growth thrives outside the comfort zone, you boldly step into situations that stretch your abilities and broaden your horizons. This audacious approach allows you to expand your skills, setting the stage for holistic advancement.

HARNESSING THE POWER OF FEEDBACK

Feedback, often underestimated, becomes a cornerstone of your evolution. Just as a leader embodies a commitment to self-betterment, you innately internalize the importance of feedback as a mechanism for improvement. By readily embracing constructive criticism, you cause your continuous transformation, adapting to changing circumstances and honing your abilities.

GUIDED BY WISDOM

An adage resonates powerfully here:

"You are known by the company you keep."

This wisdom encapsulates your associations' profound influence on your character and achievements. Within the context of leading by example, aligning yourself with individuals who inspire and motivate serves as the foundation for this facet of leadership.

DRAWING INSPIRATION FROM MODELS

By emulating positive attributes exhibited by these inspiring figures, you organically incorporate these qualities into your actions. For instance, effective time management comes to life through association with those who excel in this realm. Adopting their practices enhances your skill in optimizing time allocation, creating a ripple effect on your overall efficiency.

CULTIVATING LEADERSHIP TRAITS

Similarly, the ability to articulate intricate problem-solving approaches and master clear communication stems from the templates provided by mentors. Learning from their actions, you embody these skills, fostering a leadership style that resonates with effectiveness and influence.

EMBRACING RESILIENCE AND ADAPTABILITY

A core pillar of leading by example is cultivating resilience and adaptability. These attributes empower leaders to confront and conquer the obstacles that come their way. Resilience grants the strength to withstand setbacks, while adaptability equips them to maneuver through changing circumstances. This combination fosters a proactive mindset that thrives in the face of adversity.

REINVENTING COPING MECHANISMS

> *"Insanity is doing the same thing repeatedly and expecting different results."*
>
> —Albert Einstein

The quote underscores the necessity of evolution. Leaders recognize that progress hinges on breaking from repetitive patterns and developing fresh strategies. To conquer challenges, individuals must innovate their approaches, drawing inspiration from the successful practices of others. They craft novel coping mechanisms that lead to more favorable outcomes.

GUIDING THROUGH EXAMPLE

In pursuing growth and adaptation, leaders inspire by setting an illustrative precedent. As they reinvent their coping mechanisms, they offer a blueprint for others to follow. Witnessing a leader's resilience and willingness to embrace change, the team gains the confidence to step beyond their comfort zones. This emulation propels not only individual growth but also collective progress.

ENCOURAGING OTHERS TO FOLLOW

As leaders lead with resilience and adaptability, they become beacons for others. Their actions, born out of reinvention and courage, motivate team members to embrace change and navigate challenges head-on. The ripple effect of their example encourages a culture of innovation, fostering an environment where setbacks are transformed into stepping stones toward advancement.

In this exploration of cultivating exemplary leadership, we delve into the multifaceted nature of leading through different traits and how these qualities inspire growth and innovation on an individual and collective level.[24]

EXTENDING THE STRIDE OF LEADERSHIP

An integral part of effective leadership lies in empowering others to embrace the concept of extending their stride through incremental improvement. This concept encapsulates that consistent, small advancements, often called the "1% improvement," can collectively lead to significant progress.

As a leader, guiding others to internalize and apply this philosophy enhances their individual growth and fosters a culture of continuous enhancement within society.

24 https://www.runn.io/blog/how-to-lead-by-example

Leading by example entails personal advancement and inspiring others to adopt a similar mindset. Encouraging others to embark on a journey of 1% improvement emphasizes the significance of consistently striving for minor, manageable enhancements.

This approach is grounded in the understanding that grand achievements are often the result of sustained, incremental progress. Breaking down monumental goals into manageable components makes the daunting achievable, and motivation remains sustained.

In a workplace, a leader should encourage others to extend their stride and instill a culture of growth within the organization. The collective impact is profound when each team member commits to minor yet consistent improvements. This mindset fosters an environment where everyone is engaged in personal and professional development, propelling the organization toward enhanced productivity and innovation.

As a leader, your role is not only to set an example but also to nurture the potential of each team member. By advocating for the philosophy of 1% improvement, you demonstrate your commitment to their growth.

Encourage open discussions about progress, provide resources for skill development, and celebrate the milestones achieved through these incremental steps. Your unwavering support and guidance reinforce the message that continuous growth is valued and rewarded.

The concept of 1% improvement is a powerful tool for breaking the cycle of complacency. Often, individuals become accustomed to their comfort zones, inhibiting growth and innovation.

By urging your team to embrace minor improvements on a daily basis, you challenge them to step beyond these confines and reach for higher levels of excellence. This shift in mindset encourages proactive engagement with learning and change.

Empowering others to extend their stride through the philosophy of 1% improvement is a testament to transformative leadership. Leaders create an environment where personal and collective progress is celebrated and pursued by fostering a culture that values continuous growth and encourages incremental advancements.

This approach aligns with the principles of leading by example, showcasing that the journey of leadership is not solely about personal accomplishments but also about elevating the capabilities and achievements of the entire team.

EMBRACING MARGINAL GAINS FOR LASTING SUCCESS

In a world often captivated by the allure of rapid success, the wisdom of pursuing marginal gains emerges as a valuable alternative. While Malcolm Gladwell famously advocated that becoming world-class requires investing around 10,000 hours, the concept extends beyond sheer quantity. The crux lies in the hours invested and the quality and precision of performance during those hours. In essence, the philosophy of marginal gains underscores those significant accomplishments stem from consistent and correct effort rather than swift but subpar endeavors.

THE MYTH OF INSTANT SUCCESS

The quest for quick riches is pervasive, fostering a belief that success can be attained overnight. However, this approach often needs to pay more attention to the nuanced reality that genuine expertise and excellence necessitate time and persistent effort.

Gladwell's "10,000-hour rule" is not an exact science. It condenses the notion that greatness is achieved through a cumulative commitment to refining skills over an extended period. Yet, the critical factor is the duration spent and the caliber of practice and performance during those hours.

QUALITY OVER QUANTITY

The essence of marginal gains lies in the principle that minor, incremental improvements, when aggregated, yield remarkable results. It acknowledges that striving for mastery involves consistently honing one's abilities and making little but steady advancements.

The idea here is that it's not the isolated grand efforts that define success but the ongoing journey of refining and perfecting one's craft. Every minute spent in deliberate practice, focusing on doing things right, contributes to a bank of expertise that eventually leads to exceptional outcomes.

OPTIMIZING PERFORMANCE

While the sum of 10,000 hours serves as a symbolic benchmark, the true essence is in pursuing correct and proper performance. Spending 10,000 hours ineffectively does little to foster growth; the intentional pursuit of excellence during those hours catalyzes progress.

Marginal gain's philosophy emphasizes that every minute devoted to meaningful, focused practice enhances skills, knowledge, and performance. Thus, the hours invested become stepping stones toward proficiency and mastery.

IMPACT ON PERSONAL AND PROFESSIONAL SPHERES

Promoting the philosophy of marginal gains extends beyond individual development and permeates the professional landscape. Embracing this approach, individuals and teams recognize that consistent, thoughtful improvement results in transformative change over time. This philosophy encourages self-discipline and an organizational culture that values continuous growth and learning.

In a world enamored with shortcuts and instant gratification, the philosophy of marginal gains serves as a beacon of sustainable success. It reminds us that every small step forward, driven by intentional practice and correct execution, contributes to a journey of excellence. Whether applied individually or within a professional context, the philosophy of marginal gains underscores the power of dedicated improvement that ultimately leads to lasting accomplishments.

CULTIVATING A CULTURE OF CONTINUOUS LEARNING

> *"Leadership is not just about giving energy...it's unleashing other people's energy."*
>
> —Paul Polman

According to the principles of leading by example and embracing marginal gains, the role of fostering an environment for continuous learning and skill development comes to the forefront. This essential component requires unwavering fortitude to seek avenues that facilitate personal and professional growth actively. It involves pursuing educational materials, training opportunities, and knowledge sharing within personal and professional circles.

Fortitude emerges as the driving force behind creating an atmosphere that values and promotes continuous learning. This involves the relentless pursuit of knowledge and skill enhancement. By proactively seeking learning opportunities, individuals pave the way for their advancement. They recognize that growth is an ongoing journey and remain open to new insights that refine their abilities.

Pursuing knowledge goes beyond mere desire; it's about actively seeking educational materials, workshops, and training sessions. This proactive approach reflects a commitment to personal development. Whether reading books, enrolling in online courses, or attending seminars, dedication to learning is an investment that pays dividends in the form of increased competence and adaptability.

Encouraging an environment of continuous learning extends to leveraging the power of peer-to-peer interactions. Individuals recognize that knowledge sharing is a two-way street. Engaging in discussions and exchanging insights with friends and professional acquaintances amplifies the learning experience. This collaborative approach deepens one's understanding and exposes them to diverse perspectives, enriching their skill set.

Through fortitude-driven actions, individuals contribute to the creation of learning communities. These communities, whether online forums or local meetups, provide platforms for individuals to engage with like-minded individuals. These communities' discussions, debates, and knowledge-sharing sessions foster collective growth and intellectual stimulation.

The essence of fortitude lies in the never-ending quest for growth. Those who embrace continuous learning understand that every interaction, every piece of information, and every learning opportunity is a stepping stone toward personal enrichment. By remaining open to new ideas and actively seeking ways to expand their skill set, individuals embark on a cycle of growth that transcends limitations.

In a world of constant change and evolution, fortitude is the beacon guiding individuals toward personal and professional growth. Individuals embark on a journey of self-improvement that knows no bounds by creating an environment that prioritizes continuous learning, seeking educational resources, and fostering peer-to-peer learning.

This tactic aligns seamlessly with the principles of leading by example and the philosophy of marginal gains, reinforcing that leadership and success are built upon a foundation of unwavering dedication to growth and knowledge.

A CYCLICAL JOURNEY OF GROWTH

Central to the idea of "*Lengthen Your Stride*" is a dynamic cycle that fuels continuous professional enhancement. This perpetual loop hinges on the power of feedback, interwoven with celebrations of achievements at every step of the journey. By fostering a culture of self-incentivization and recognition, this approach creates a profound impact not only on individual growth but also on the collective elevation of those within your sphere of influence.

ENGINE OF EVOLUTION

At the heart of this journey lies the continual loop of feedback. This iterative process involves seeking input from mentors, peers and self-assessment to uncover areas of improvement. Feedback provides the critical insight needed to identify strengths to be fortified and weaknesses to be addressed. The humility to receive feedback and the wisdom to implement it drive a perpetual evolution toward professional excellence.

The *Lengthen Your Stride* philosophy rejects the notion of waiting until the finish line to celebrate. Instead, it advocates for celebrating every stride along the path to improvement. Each step forward, no matter how small, deserves recognition. By acknowledging these incremental successes, individuals not only bolster their motivation but also cultivate a culture that values progress, however gradual.

The celebration is a potent incentive that propels individual and collective growth. By celebrating accomplishments, individuals reinforce their commitment to their objectives. This self-incentivization, driven by positive reinforcement, fuels the desire to persist in facing challenges. Similarly, this behavior ripples through interpersonal interactions, inspiring others to pursue their goals with renewed vigor.

Celebrating achievements, no matter their scale, weaves a web of appreciation. This appreciation extends to the self and radiates outward to those who contribute to one's journey. A culture of mutual respect and recognition flourishes by demonstrating the value placed on every endeavor. This "bubble" envelops individuals, fostering an environment that cherishes both the individual contributions and the collaborative efforts of the community.

The synergy of feedback, celebration, and continuous improvement creates an ecosystem where growth thrives. This dynamic interplay nurtures a culture of striving for excellence while celebrating progress. It's not just about the final destination but about the transformative journey. The commitment to improvement resonates in the professional realm, driving individuals to stretch their capabilities and enrich their accomplishments.

The cycle of feedback and celebration, at the heart of *Lengthen Your Stride*, forms a potent recipe for enduring professional growth. By embracing continuous improvement, acknowledging achievements, and incentivizing progress, individuals construct a path toward impactful and fulfilling success.

This philosophy goes beyond personal development. It profoundly impacts the collective spirit, fostering an ecosystem where contributions are treasured, celebrated, and rewarded.

FOUNDATIONS OF AUTHENTIC LEADERSHIP

Elevating one's leadership presence involves a critical step: building trust and establishing rapport with friends, colleagues, and clients. Authenticity, genuine connections, and transparent communication guide this endeavor. The ability to convey dependability and consistency in actions further cements the foundation of authentic leadership. This approach enhances relationships and fosters an open communication environment, echoing the principles previously discussed within the narrative.

Authenticity is the cornerstone of forging strong connections and inspiring trust. By embracing your true self and revealing vulnerability, you create a space where others can relate to you genuinely. Authenticity eradicates the façade of pretense, enabling individuals to connect with you as a person rather than merely as a leader. This genuine portrayal is the first step toward establishing bonds built on trust.

Honest and open communication is one of the most potent avenues to build trust and rapport. Transparent conversations, devoid of hidden agendas, cultivate a sense of reliability. Colleagues and clients gravitate toward leaders who offer unfiltered insights and treat information sharing as a sign of respect and trust. This transparent approach underscores that you value their perspectives, fostering a two-way flow of ideas and understanding.

Trust is a fragile commodity that flourishes when supported by dependability and consistency. Demonstrating that your words align with your actions creates a sense of reliability. Colleagues and clients observe you follow through on commitments and stand by your promises. This consistency establishes a sense of security, knowing they can rely on you in smooth sailing and challenging times.

The cultivation of trust and rapport is closely intertwined with the promotion of open communication. Authentic leadership entails creating an environment where honesty is the norm and conversations are free from hidden agendas. This open dialogue facilitates a deeper understanding of shared goals, challenges, and aspirations. Through the lens of transparent communication, a culture of mutual trust and respect flourishes.

The journey of building trust and rapport echoes the overarching principles discussed within the narrative. Authenticity aligns with the philosophy of leading by example, as both underscore the value of embracing one's true self.

Transparent communication resonates with the philosophy of marginal gains, highlighting the significance of incremental but consistent improvements. Dependability mirrors the cycle of feedback and celebration, emphasizing the importance of steady growth and recognition.

For authentic leadership, the ability to build trust and connection is a pivotal skill. By fostering authentic relationships through transparent communication, consistency, and genuine connections, leaders create a foundation of trust that fortifies interactions with friends, colleagues, and clients. This trust, carefully nurtured, enhances collaboration and engagement and amplifies the collective potential for success within the professional sphere.

FEEDBACK LOOP OF ACTIVE LISTENING

A feedback loop nurtured by active listening is embedded within the fabric of effective leadership. Active listening, a cornerstone of authentic engagement, serves a dual purpose: understanding and demonstrating genuine interest in shared information. This cycle of attentive listening fosters understanding and cultivates open communication, leading to the discovery of strategies for issue resolution and growth.

Active listening transcends passive reception; it embodies a proactive effort to comprehend the information conveyed. You acknowledge the significance of their message by genuinely tuning in to the speaker's words, tone, and non-verbal cues. This empathetic engagement demonstrates your willingness to learn and cements a connection based on mutual respect.

Active listening lays the foundation for an environment of open communication. Engaging in meaningful conversations characterized by genuine interest creates a space where ideas, concerns, and feedback can flow freely. This culture of openness provides a fertile ground for collaboration, problem-solving, and fostering stronger relationships.

Open communication, nurtured through active listening, becomes a linchpin for issue resolution. As you immerse yourself in dialogues, you absorb insights and perspectives that contribute to resolving challenges. This echoes the earlier point about modeling behaviors; by actively listening and engaging in meaningful exchanges, you absorb strategies and tools that facilitate effective problem-solving.

The strategies and tools gathered through active listening form a toolkit for addressing challenges. When you engage in open communication and actively listen to others, you gain insights into approaching and navigating issues. This is a powerful manifestation of the leadership principle of leading by example – by immersing yourself in these interactions, you embody the behavior you wish to encourage in others.

This feedback loop of active listening, open communication, and issue resolution embodies a seamless interplay of principles. Active listening represents the authenticity and transparency of leading by example, demonstrating your commitment to understanding and mutual growth.

The feedback loop of active listening encapsulates the multi-faceted nature of leadership. It's a conduit for understanding, a compound for open communication, and a reservoir of strategies for issue resolution.[25]

As you actively listen, you model behaviors that ripple through the organization, fostering an environment of empathy, understanding, and progress. This approach, deeply intertwined with the core principles of leadership, exemplifies the power of engaged and authentic interactions in shaping an environment of growth and success.

EMPOWERING THROUGH DELEGATION

Viewed through the lens of celebration and personal relationships, the leadership journey unfolds with a natural change to help others improve. The most potent avenue for fostering improvement is delegation – the strategic division of tasks and re-

25 https://publicrelations.ucmerced.edu/writing-and-editing/internal-communications/listening-and-feedback

sponsibilities. This deliberate action underscores your belief in others' capacities while allowing autonomy and trust to flourish.

The art of delegation unlocks the potential of team members, facilitating their ownership of responsibilities and encouraging optimal performance.

Just as a team player in sports assumes distinct roles, every member of an organization has responsibilities to shoulder. Delegation embodies your belief in their abilities to perform these roles. You convey confidence in their capabilities by entrusting them with specific tasks. This empowerment doesn't just cultivate growth; it cements a sense of shared purpose and collective contribution.

Entrustment transcends the mere division of tasks; it provides team members with autonomy and trust. When individuals are given ownership of their responsibilities, they are motivated to perform at their best. This trust amplifies their commitment and accountability, as they recognize that their actions contribute directly to the team's success. The autonomy afforded through delegation further encourages creativity and innovative problem-solving.

Delegation doesn't merely allocate tasks; it's a strategic effort to tap into the strengths and skills of team members. By recognizing their unique attributes, you can assign tasks that align with their abilities, fostering efficiency and job satisfaction.

The notion of optimal performance is often misconstrued as perfection. However, the philosophy of 1% improvement dispels this notion. Optimal performance, in this context, embraces iterative growth. It celebrates the idea that consistent, incremental advancements lead to continuous improvement. This approach is grounded in the understanding that pursuing excellence is an ongoing journey, not a destination.

Delegation isn't merely about task assignments; it's an avenue to learning about people. Through this process, you gain insights into the strengths and preferences of team members. This knowledge empowers you to facilitate an environment where each individual's capabilities are harnessed effectively. It underscores the importance of continuous learning, open communication, and personalized engagement.

PROMOTING AN ENVIRONMENT OF RESPONSIBILITY AND COLLABORATION

This journey toward effective leadership unfolds with the cultivation of responsibility and collaboration. This pivotal stage is marked by clear expectations and strategic guidance, forming the bedrock of a collaborative and productive environment. As communication threads weave through this fabric, roles become interdependent and integral within a professional, business, or social circle.

Central to this phase is the imparting of clear expectations and focused guidance. These elements serve as the compass, directing team members toward their roles and responsibilities. This clarity empowers individuals to comprehend their contributions within the larger framework, reinforcing the value of their role in achieving collective goals.

The understanding of roles extends beyond individual tasks. It encompasses the web of interdependencies within a team. Each role is not isolated but intricately connected to the functions of others. This interplay underscores the essence of teamwork and collaboration. Acknowledging that every contribution is a piece of a giant puzzle fosters a sense of collective ownership and commitment.

Responsibility emerges as a natural byproduct of this environment. The interwoven threads of guidance, clear expectations, and role understanding converge to create a culture of ownership. Team members feel a sense of accountability, not just for their tasks but for the overall success of the endeavor. This responsibility is nurtured within the cocoon of mutual trust and shared goals.

The heart of this environment is collaborative communication. Team members communicate openly, sharing goals, timelines, and requirements. This open dialogue creates a collective understanding that transcends individual perspectives. Collaborative communication promotes alignment, cohesion, and a shared sense of purpose, amplifying the synergistic potential of the team.

Throughout this journey, the loop of feedback remains ever-present. It's the invisible thread that connects every facet of leadership. As responsibilities are assumed, expectations met, and collaborative efforts forged, feedback fuels the evolution of each component. The instrument ensures that the process is dynamic, adaptable, and constantly evolving.

At its core, this leadership chapter underscores two truths. First, the journey is one of perpetual improvement, a commitment to improving with each step. Second, it champions the art of effective communication, rooted in clarity, guidance, and collaborative spirit. By intertwining these principles, a dynamic environment takes shape, where growth becomes a collective endeavor, and success is measured in individual achievements and the progress of the entire team.

The culmination of responsibility and collaboration creates an ecosystem of collective efficacy. This web, woven with guidance, expectation, and cooperation, symbolizes leadership's ability to nurture an environment that thrives on shared objectives and mutual growth. As expectations are met, roles are understood, and communication flourishes, the spirit of continuous improvement thrives, elevating individual capabilities and the team's overall potential.

IMPACTFUL DEMONSTRATION OF LEADERSHIP

In the documentary "Pumping Iron," Arnold Schwarzenegger's approach to leadership provides a powerful example of how individuals can inspire and foster growth within a community. Through his actions and interactions, Schwarzenegger illustrates the capacity to create a feedback loop of motivation, responsibility, collaboration, and accountability among fellow bodybuilders.

CREATING A FEEDBACK LOOP

Schwarzenegger's early realization was that he could catalyze others' growth by encouraging them to join him in the gym. This simple act created a feedback loop where his commitment to exercise and self-improvement inspired others to join in. This loop thrived on mutual motivation, where each person's progress fed into the others', creating a continuous cycle of encouragement and advancement.

EMPOWERING RESPONSIBILITY

Central to Schwarzenegger's leadership was the notion of personal responsibility. By inviting others to share in his journey, he demonstrated his dedication and ignited a sense of accountability within each individual. Each person recognized that their progress was in their own hands, and this ownership empowered them to strive for their goals with renewed vigor.

COLLABORATIVE REINFORCEMENT

The community formed around Schwarzenegger in the gym exemplified the concept of self-enforcing collaboration. The shared journey forged a bond that extended beyond mere acquaintanceship. These bodybuilders understood that their combined efforts were mutually reinforcing. They recognized that working together could amplify their results and achieve their objectives more effectively.

COMMUNICATION AND ACCOUNTABILITY

Within this environment, communication and accountability flourished. Schwarzenegger's presence cultivated open dialogue and instilled a sense of personal responsibility. Individuals understood that even though they were accountable to themselves, their commitment was visible to their peers. This mutual accountability created an atmosphere of shared commitment, where each person's progress reflected their dedication.

LEADERSHIP ROLE THROUGH EXAMPLE

Schwarzenegger's leadership role wasn't defined by formal instruction or authority. Instead, it emerged from the inspiration he provided through his actions. He demonstrated leadership by showing the way in physical training and fostering an environment of growth, mutual support, and continuous improvement. His leadership was rooted in leading by example, creating a ripple effect that touched every community member.

Arnold Schwarzenegger's influence in "Pumping Iron" transcends the realm of bodybuilding. His leadership model showcases the power of inspiration, shared responsibility, collaboration, and accountability. His actions exemplify how genuine leadership doesn't necessarily rely on titles or formal roles. Instead, it's about creating an environment where individuals are motivated, empowered, and responsible for their growth. Schwarzenegger's journey is a testament to the impact of leading by example and fostering a community of collective ambition.

CONCLUSION

THIS CHAPTER TOOK US ON A VOYAGE THROUGH THE INTRICATE FABric of leadership, unveiling its multifaceted character and extensive influence. We embarked on our journey by uncovering the simplicity and profundity of leading by example, where even the smallest, consistent actions radiate as sources of inspiration. Progressing onward, we plunged into empowering others to embrace the potency of 1% improvements, acknowledging how the collective impact stems from individual strides.

Our exploration flowed seamlessly into trust-building and the cultivation of meaningful connections—a cornerstone of impactful leadership. Through trust, bonds are solidified and collaborations fortified, ushering in shared achievements and collective development.

As the chapter unfolded, we traversed the dynamic landscape of delegation and team management. Here, we gleaned that a true leader operates like a conductor, harmonizing the distinctive strengths of team members to craft a symphony of accomplishments. A consistent theme emerged—leadership transcends mere actions, encapsulating values and principles. It's about guidance, inspiration, and empowerment reverberating across all facets of existence, spanning the professional domain and far beyond.

As we draw this chapter to a close, let's remember that leadership isn't confined to a label or a role—it's a daily choice, a commitment to evolution, and a dedication to uplifting others. Whether manifested through our consistent acts, the gradual strides we motivate, the bonds we nurture, or the teams we steward, leadership interweaves with them all. It creates a harmonious composition that molds our vocations and the core of our identity.

PART 4

BUSINESS AND ENTREPRENEURSHIP

CHAPTER EIGHT

INNOVATION AND GROWTH

The dynamic business landscape constantly changes, challenging even the most seasoned leaders. From altering national regulations on pay fairness and workforce categorization to shifts in the job market that make talent acquisition more demanding, leaders have a lot to contend with.

Within numerous internal and external variables, prioritization becomes a struggle. Managing day-to-day operations is daunting, especially with economic issues like inflation and external pressures such as meeting customer and stakeholder expectations.

Guiding an organization toward progress through novel strategies like generative AI, innovative employee training modules, and transitioning to cloud infrastructure can be overwhelming, potentially leading to mistakes.

CEOs must drastically change their operational approaches to ensure ongoing success in today's corporate world. The pandemic has also prompted employees to reconsider their purpose and career paths.

On the other hand, consumers are pondering whether to remain loyal to companies during significant disruptions. As the global economy reshapes its functioning, this has opened up fresh prospects for leaders who prioritize their workforce and customers to adapt successfully without losing momentum.

Significant transformations have shaped the business landscape in recent years, and each day brings news of companies grappling to stay current. The surge of the freelance economy, the influence of technology on businesses, shifts in consumer habits, and, more recently, alterations in the economic terrain have all played their part.

Navigating change stands as a formidable task in business management. Companies must continually adjust to remain pertinent, whether it entails economic shifts, emerging regulations, or evolving customer tastes. How can you guarantee that your business can endure these challenges and emerge triumphant?

The crux of this situation lies in recognizing the profound opportunity that arises from acknowledging the perpetual nature of change. There's wisdom in understanding that change is the sole constant.

> *"Change is the only constant in life."*
>
> —Heraclitus

This profound insight resonates deeply with the essence of the business world's dynamics. It serves as a reminder that adaptation is an intrinsic part of progress, an integral strategy for businesses to flourish. In a world where shifts in technology, economic paradigms, and consumer behaviors are routine, accepting and welcoming change is a cornerstone for sustained success.

In an environment characterized by constant flux, the key to success lies in adapting and embracing change. Rather than resisting or fearing it, businesses can find resilience by learning to navigate the shifting tides. This mindset shift is not just about survival but about seizing opportunities. Businesses that recognize change as an integral part of growth position themselves to proactively innovate, evolve, and excel. Such companies weather storms effectively and capitalize on the winds of change to propel themselves forward.

This outlook cultivates a proactive stance, encouraging businesses to anticipate, prepare for, and initiate change. By fostering a culture that celebrates innovation, experimentation, and learning, companies position themselves to navigate the ever-changing currents of the business landscape. The capacity to evolve becomes a competitive advantage, allowing them to capitalize on emerging opportunities rather than merely responding to challenges.

By recognizing change as an intrinsic facet of the business landscape and embracing it, companies position themselves to harness its power to their advantage. In a world where the only constant is change, the ability to adapt becomes the foundation for enduring success and sustained growth.

EMBRACING CHANGE AND INNOVATION

> *"The biggest risk is not taking any risk. In a world that is changing quickly, the only strategy guaranteed to fail is not taking risks."*
>
> —Mark Zuckerberg

HUMANS TEND TO BE CREATURES OF HABIT, GRAVITATING TOWARD routines and patterns while often resisting change. This inclination is especially evident in business, where many organizations and individuals persist in their familiar ways, even when these no longer yield effective results. However, to achieve different outcomes in your business, adopting change and exploring novel avenues is essential. Remember the famous quote:

> *"Insanity is doing the same thing repeatedly and expecting different results."*
>
> —Albert Einstein

This idea underscores the futility of expecting change when adhering to the status quo. Though Einstein's remark wasn't about business, its wisdom resonates across contexts. Divergent results necessitate the willingness to experiment with different strategies. A common reason for resistance to change is the unease and uncertainty it brings. Familiarity breeds comfort, yet it's crucial to acknowledge that personal growth and advancement often stem from venturing beyond the comfort zone. By embracing change and venturing into uncharted territories, you expand your horizons, cultivate new skills, and uncover innovative solutions.

Change isn't just beneficial in the business world—it's imperative. Markets, technologies, and customer demands are in perpetual flux. To retain competitiveness and relevance, adaptation is paramount. This entails embracing fresh concepts, taking calculated risks, and engaging in experimentation. Netflix exemplifies this mindset; starting as a DVD rental service in 1997, the company transitioned to online streaming to meet evolving demands, now boasting over 200 million global subscribers.

Similarly, Amazon's journey began as an online bookstore in 1994. Founder Jeff Bezos, foreseeing the potential of e-commerce, diversified the company to encompass an extensive array of goods and services. Amazon is one of the world's largest retailers, valued at approximately $1 trillion. These instances demonstrate a readiness to embrace change and experiment with innovative paths. Rather than clinging to outdated models, these companies assumed risk and ventured into new territories.

Indeed, change isn't always effortless. Departing from familiar routines and embracing novelty can be a daunting endeavor. Yet, the rewards of adapting, evolving, and embracing change are substantial, often leading to newfound successes and growth.

ART OF STAYING INFORMED AND PROACTIVE

"To be successful, you have to have your heart in your business and your business in your heart."

—Thomas Watson Sr.

The key to effectively navigating the ever-changing landscape is anticipating and devising strategies to respond to shifts. This involves a proactive approach centered around staying well-informed and actively participating in society's dynamic currents. Active engagement with the evolving world is crucial in a world where distraction can often pull attention away.

Staying informed goes beyond mere surface-level awareness. It requires a deep immersion in current affairs, market trends, and societal developments. This process involves more than just seeking a momentary distraction; it entails being attuned to the pulse of change. Especially in industries or sectors subject to rapid transformations, such as technology or fashion, staying ahead of the curve is not a luxury but a necessity.

Being part of society, understanding the nuances of markets, and perceiving the subtleties of emerging trends are the building blocks of successful adaptation. Industries are interwoven with the fabric of society, responding to shifts in consumer preferences, technological advancements, and economic fluctuations. By actively participating in this ecosystem, business leaders position themselves to seize emerging opportunities, not just react to challenges.

Numerous resources are available to aid in this endeavor. Countless articles and publications dissect market trends, emerging technologies, and societal shifts. Engaging with these resources can provide invaluable insights into the direction of industries. This knowledge guides decision-making, enabling leaders to navigate the complex waters of change with more confidence.

Actively participating in staying informed and engaged is a strategic investment in the future. It is a means of embracing change, anticipating its effects, and forging a path to thrive amidst uncertainty. Just as a captain studies the weather to navigate the seas, a business leader must stay attuned to the currents of change to steer their enterprise toward enduring success.

Gaining a comprehensive grasp of the evolving landscape involves active engagement through avenues such as attending conferences and participating in networking events. These opportunities provide invaluable platforms for individuals to keep abreast of changes, fostering a broader understanding of shifts and trends. These interactions are not confined to specific regions. They occur in every city and state, with many networking prospects, many of which are cost-effective or even free. Additionally, while significant conferences may require an investment, the knowledge and insights acquired make them worthwhile.

Conferences and networking events function as knowledge hubs where professionals from diverse industries converge to share insights, exchange ideas, and forecast industry trends. These gatherings serve as windows into the world of innovation, offering glimpses of emerging technologies, transformative business models, and shifts in consumer behavior. Engaging with experts and thought leaders enables attendees to glean firsthand information, transcending the boundaries of traditional learning methods.

Participating in local networking events can be particularly impactful. These events facilitate connections with fellow professionals, entrepreneurs, and thought leaders within your vicinity. These interactions offer an exchange of perspectives, enabling participants to gauge the pulse of their industry's transformation on a grassroots level. Moreover, attending these events can uncover local trends and market nuances that might not be evident from a broader perspective.

While some conferences come with a financial commitment, the investment often pales compared to the insights gained. These events gather industry luminaries and pioneers, unveiling cutting-edge concepts and strategies that can reshape businesses. Exposure to different viewpoints and the opportunity to engage in thought-provoking discussions can spark new ideas and inspire creative problem-solving.

In a world of constant change, the commitment to staying informed through conferences and networking events becomes a strategic imperative. These experiences catalyze growth, inspire innovation, and foster a deeper understanding of the dynamic forces at play. Whether through local meetups or large-scale conferences, embracing these opportunities ensures that individuals remain at the forefront of change, primed to leverage it for success.[26]

LEADERSHIP'S ROLE IN ADOPTING CHANGE

Embedded within this dynamic lies a crucial facet of leadership: leaders' responsibility for their teams. Leadership extends beyond steering the ship; it fosters an environment where individuals can thrive and contribute to collective growth. Leaders serve as custodians of their people, nurturing their professional development and enabling them to participate actively in the ever-evolving business landscape.

In this context, leaders become more than just decision-makers; they emerge as enablers of knowledge dissemination. Encouraging a culture of open sharing within their organizations becomes paramount. The flow of knowledge and expertise on market trends and developments should not be confined to a select few. Leaders must advocate for a culture where insights are freely shared, and information is democratized, allowing each team member to contribute and benefit.

The role of leaders extends to encouraging their teams to participate in these gatherings collectively. These events cease to be mere networking opportunities; they transform into collaborative forums for growth. By attending as a cohesive unit, teams can collectively absorb and analyze information, generating multifaceted perspectives that can illuminate strategic pathways. This group engagement fosters a sense of shared mission and camaraderie, amplifying the overall impact of these experiences.

Leaders who champion the importance of attending conferences and networking events underscore their commitment to

26 https://auxipress.be/en/being-well-informed-before-anyone-else-why-is-it-essential-for-brands/

the organization's progression. They communicate that staying informed is a personal endeavor and a collective journey. This perspective cultivates a sense of unity and collective learning that is indispensable in a rapidly changing environment.

The leadership component is nurturing a culture of continuous learning and shared exploration. By empowering teams to share knowledge and attend events collectively, leaders create a dynamic ecosystem that is agile, adaptable, and primed to embrace change. In this way, leadership drives organizational resilience, growth, and success in constant transformation.

CRAFTING DYNAMIC STRATEGIES

Once embracing change becomes a fundamental stance, coupled with the commitment to staying informed, the next step is to formulate strategies. These strategies serve as navigational tools through the evolving landscape. They assess the impending changes and facilitate evolution alongside these shifts. The ultimate objective is to integrate these changes into the emerging paradigm seamlessly.

Strategizing involves a multi-pronged approach. It encompasses identifying upcoming changes, proactively adapting to them, and their eventual integration into the evolving framework. This process isn't static; it reflects an ongoing mindset centered around change and adaptability. Each strategy is a building block contributing to a bigger picture of resilience and progress.

As the threads of staying informed and embracing change converge, these strategies acquire their potency. Staying actively engaged with the dynamic business world equips leaders with insights that can be translated into actionable strategies. The capacity to anticipate market trends and shifts structures the bedrock for crafting practical approaches. In this landscape, conferences and networking events become pivotal as they offer glimpses into the emerging future and opportunities for collaboration.

The concept of lengthening one's stride aptly captures this journey. It embodies a philosophy of continuous improvement, where small incremental changes accumulate over time. These minor adjustments, when compounded, yield substantial impacts on how markets evolve. Just as each step taken with longer strides covers more ground, every strategic decision guided by the mindset of adaptability contributes to an organization's capacity to traverse the changing landscape.

This plan encapsulates a holistic approach to thriving in a dynamic business environment. It begins with recognizing the inevitability of change and transcends into actively engaging with market shifts. Strategies act as bridges between these elements, enabling businesses to endure and flourish despite transformations. The overarching theme of embracing change and encouraging adaptability ties all these components together, forming a robust framework for sustained success.

ENHANCING PRODUCTS AND SERVICES

Our journey progresses to the critical phase of reviewing the landscape, which leads to identifying avenues for enhancing products and services. At this juncture, the spotlight shifts to business innovation, a domain that extends beyond personal development and encompasses the evolution of offerings. This chapter in the narrative revolves around enhancing individual skills and fostering innovation and improvement in products and services.

This dimension of innovation broadens the horizon, focusing on the evolution of products and services within the context of a dynamic market. The pursuit of excellence extends beyond static notions; it's an ongoing exploration of opportunities brought forth by change. It's the art of recognizing openings for advancement and honing in on areas where product and service performance can be elevated.

Innovation is the driving force, creating a proactive culture that thrives on improvement. It's about leveraging market shifts, evolving technologies, and changing consumer needs as catalysts for innovation. This phase requires a discerning eye to pinpoint where value can be added and where existing offerings can be refined. Each alteration, each enhancement, contributes to an overall trajectory of progress.

Central to this approach is establishing a framework that facilitates identifying opportunities and quantifying their impact. The implementation of approaches that enable precise measurement and benchmarking is pivotal. This allows organizations to gauge the effectiveness of their innovation efforts, ensuring that they are aligned with tangible outcomes.

The narrative unfolds as a sequence of interconnected steps, culminating in a holistic approach to thriving in a dynamic business landscape. Staying informed, embracing change, strategizing, and reviewing the environment converges to foster continuous innovation and improvement. This narrative, underpinned by the ethos of adaptability and growth, empowers organizations to navigate change and leverage it to their advantage. It's an evolution that spans from individual mindsets to product and service offerings, fostering a culture of perpetual advancement and success.

CULTIVATING A CULTURE OF CONTINUAL IMPROVEMENT

"The only sustainable competitive advantage is an organization's ability to learn faster than the competition."

—Peter Senge

In this pivotal phase of the journey, we delve into the practical methods that underpin the ethos of constant growth and enhancement. Developing a continual improvement culture is essential for personal and professional development and serves as a cornerstone for refining products and services within the dynamic market landscape.

Innovative continuous improvement is a powerful strategy for companies to gain an edge and maintain their competitive advantage. Businesses can reduce errors, eliminate waste, and boost productivity by consistently refining processes and systems. Initially, the focus may be on resolving significant issues, but what follows once those hurdles are cleared?

To harness the full potential of continuous improvement, more than merely solving big problems is required. The subsequent step is to pinpoint opportunities that propel the business beyond survival into a flourishing realm. This phase requires a strategic approach to identifying and prioritizing areas for growth within existing processes.

STEP 1: REGULAR ASSESSMENTS AND FEEDBACK SOLICITATION

THE FIRST STRIDE TOWARD OPTIMIZATION INVOLVES CONDUCTING regular assessments of your offerings. This proactive approach ensures that you are consistently aware of the shifting dynamics and opportunities for enhancement. Additionally, actively solicit feedback from your customers and clients. Their insights are invaluable, providing an external perspective that can pinpoint areas where refinement is needed. Beyond customers, team members are also a goldmine of ideas. Encourage their input, for they interact daily with the products and services you offer, and their input can provide fresh insights.

STEP 2: IDENTIFICATION OF IMPROVEMENT AREAS

With insights gathered from customers and team members, the next step involves identifying the precise areas for improvement. Whether streamlining a product's user experience, enhancing service efficiency, or adapting to evolving customer preferences, this phase focuses on granularity. Each pinpointed area is a stepping stone toward overall enhancement.

STEP 3: IMPLEMENTATION OF INCREMENTAL CHANGES

The heart of the matter lies in implementation. The book's core principle — "lengthening your stride" — translates here as making incremental improvements. These minor but consistent adjustments accumulate to create a significant impact. It's about deliberately introducing changes that optimize products, services, and operational approaches.

STEP 4: NURTURING A CULTURE OF CONTINUAL IMPROVEMENT

Implementation isn't a one-time affair; it's a mindset. Cultivate a culture that embodies the spirit of constant growth. Encourage every team member to see themselves as contributors to a culture of improvement. This culture isn't confined to products and services alone; it extends to personal development, approaches, and team dynamics.

STEP 5: CREATING A COLLABORATIVE ENVIRONMENT

An environment that encourages and nurtures continual improvement is a collaborative one. Foster open communication, where ideas flow freely, and contributions are valued. Encourage cross-functional collaboration, where diverse perspectives combine to fuel innovation. When people feel their input matters, the seeds of improvement are sown and nurtured.

In the dynamic business landscape, embracing change and cultivating a culture of constant advancement is not just a choice but a necessity. By soliciting feedback, identifying improvement areas, implementing incremental changes, fostering a culture of growth, and nurturing a collaborative environment, you pave the way for ongoing optimization. This is the heart of the journey — a journey toward excellence through iterative and consistent improvements. As the book's theme underscores, it's about lengthening your stride, inch by inch, to create lasting impact and sustained success.[27]

FOSTERING INNOVATION AND SUSTAINING PROGRESS

In the vibrant ecosystem of a culture of continual improvement, the focus now shifts to nurturing a culture of innovation and sustaining progress. This section explores the pivotal role that communication, collaboration, recognition, measurement, and learning play in weaving a dynamic fabric of innovation.

27 https://ip.com/blog/how-to-identify-opportunities-for-improvement/

STEP 1: COMMUNICATION AND COLLABORATION AS CORNERSTONES

Communication and collaboration form the foundation of an environment of growth and improvement. Through open channels of dialogue, ideas are shared and nurtured. Collaborative efforts harness the collective intelligence of the team, amplifying innovative potential. This collaborative environment becomes a breeding ground for fresh solutions and inventive ideas.

> **Example:** At Google, the famous "20% time" policy encouraged employees to dedicate one-fifth of their work time to pursuing innovative projects unrelated to their primary roles. This policy led to many successful products, including Gmail and Google News.

STEP 2: RECOGNIZING AND REWARDING INITIATIVES

Innovation thrives when initiatives are recognized and rewarded. Individuals who bring forth novel ideas and solutions should be acknowledged and celebrated. This validates their efforts and encourages others to step forward with their contributions, fostering a culture of collective ingenuity.

> **Example:** The "Innovation Award" at 3M, known as the "Carlson Award," celebrates employees who significantly contribute to the company's growth through innovation. This recognition inspires a culture where innovation is prized and celebrated.

STEP 3: ESTABLISHING PERFORMANCE METRICS AND CULTIVATING CREATIVE PROBLEM SOLVING

Measuring innovation requires well-defined performance metrics. Create a framework that encourages and values creative problem-solving. These metrics should reflect the ability to innovate, experiment, and generate solutions that drive the organization forward.

> **Example:** Apple's "Blue Sky" program incentivizes employees to propose innovative ideas and solutions. These ideas are then reviewed and potentially developed into new products or features.

STEP 4: CULTIVATING A CULTURE OF ONGOING LEARNING AND GROWTH

Innovation thrives in an environment of continuous learning and experimentation. Establish processes that encourage ongoing education and skill enhancement. By nurturing a culture of learning, you empower your team to stay up-to-date with evolving trends and technologies.

> **Example:** Amazon's "Just Do It" program encourages employees to take ownership of their ideas and experiment with new projects. This fosters a spirit of curiosity, exploration, and growth.

As you create and foster this culture of innovation, remember that it's not a one-time feat. It's about maintaining an ongoing commitment to pushing boundaries, challenging the status quo, and embracing change. This is a perpetual discovery and advancement journey where creativity and innovation become the lifeblood of your organization's success. Through communication, collaboration, recognition, measurement, and ongoing learning, you shape an ecosystem that thrives on the power of innovative thinking and continuous improvement.[28]

EXPANDING HORIZONS WITH MARKET INSIGHTS AND STRATEGIC ALLIANCES

As we navigate the transformative landscape of continual improvement, the spotlight now shifts to an indispensable component – understanding new markets and harnessing strategic alliances. In a world where innovation and progress are intertwined, staying ahead necessitates more than just refining existing processes; it requires a profound comprehension of market dynamics and the foresight to forge partnerships that amplify impact.

UNLOCKING NEW MARKET OPPORTUNITIES

As markets evolve and shift, so do the possibilities for your products and services. Understanding how emerging markets may impact your offerings is crucial. Market trends and customer needs become guiding lights. Through vigilant market research and analysis, you identify avenues ripe for growth.

The best example is when Apple recognized the growing demand for wearable technology and capitalized on the trend by introducing the Apple Watch. This strategic move tapped into a new market segment and expanded its product portfolio.

LEVERAGING EXISTING STRENGTHS FOR NEW VENTURES:

The bridge between your present achievements and future successes lies in your personal and professional strengths. Your ex-

28 https://www.kainexus.com/continuous-improvement/best-practices-for-continuous-improvement/opportunities-for-improvement

pertise and organizational capabilities can be the foundation for venturing into new markets and developing innovative products. Adapt your strengths to new contexts, paving the way for expansion.

Just like Tesla's venture into energy storage solutions aligned with its expertise in electric vehicles. By leveraging their existing strengths, they entered a new market and became a significant player in renewable energy storage.

CULTIVATING STRATEGIC PARTNERSHIPS AND COLLABORATIONS

The power of strategic partnerships is immeasurable. Collaborations extend your influence, enhance market presence and fuel exponential growth. Combining resources, knowledge, and networks amplifies your reach and drives innovation.

Remember the partnership between Starbucks and Spotify that brought together the coffee giant's customer base with the music streaming platform's users? This collaboration enhanced the customer experience and expanded both brands' reach.

In this era of dynamic change, embracing continual improvement is a journey of multifaceted dimensions. It's not limited to internal processes; it encompasses understanding market shifts, leveraging strengths, and creating collaborative synergies. By actively pursuing new market opportunities, adapting to emerging trends, and forging strategic alliances, your organization propels forward with the momentum of innovation and impact. Through this journey, the improvement ethos transcends boundaries, becoming a beacon for sustained excellence and prosperity.

CONCLUSION

THE CURRENTS OF CHANGE AND INNOVATION ARE CEASELESS IN THE vast expanse of the business world. As we embarked on this chapter, we explored the dynamic landscape businesses navigate daily, where evolution is not an option but a necessity. The very essence of success lies in the ability to harness change as a force for growth.

At the helm of our journey, we illuminated the significance of embracing change. Adapting to the ever-shifting market is not a mere choice but a strategic imperative. Those who flourish are the ones who understand that every twist and turn brings forth opportunities waiting to be seized.

In our quest for excellence, we dissected the art of identifying those opportunities, honing in on the nooks and crannies where products and services can shine brighter. The spotlight shifted to the heart of organizational progress: a culture of continuous improvement. In this culture, ideas find their wings, and innovation becomes the pulse of daily operations.

Guided by the stars of expansion and foresight, we ventured into new markets, discovering the power of synergy through collaborations and strategic alliances. Each step is a testament to the unwavering commitment to growth.

As we dock in the harbor of this chapter's conclusion, let us reflect on the wisdom gleaned from this journey. The business landscape may be ever-evolving, but armed with the strategies unveiled here, we stand fortified against the tides of change. The power to survive and thrive lies within those who embrace change, seek opportunity, foster improvement, and boldly venture into uncharted waters.

CHAPTER NINE

ORGANIZATIONAL EFFICIENCY

The ultimate aspiration of every business is to become the foremost choice for products or services, marked by consistent and timely deliveries of top-tier quality. The vision is to garner customer admiration and foster unwavering motivation among employees, propelling the business toward the zenith of success.

However, this lofty dream remains a fantasy if a critical aspect is addressed: enhancing operational efficiency. This essential component is the linchpin that transforms ambitions into tangible reality. Without an unwavering focus on improving efficiency, pursuing excellence becomes an unattainable ideal.

Operational efficiency encompasses streamlining processes, optimizing resource allocation, and eliminating wastage. The engine drives a business toward cost-effectiveness, enhanced productivity, and impeccable quality. When operations are executed with precision and finesse, the result is a seamless workflow that positively impacts the bottom line and customer satisfaction.

In today's competitive landscape, operational efficiency is not merely a choice; it's a necessity. It distinguishes successful businesses from those that falter under the weight of inefficiencies. Businesses can navigate challenges, seize opportunities, and adapt swiftly to dynamic market demands by prioritizing efficiency.

Efficiency is a universal goal for all companies, yet a proper understanding of its essence still needs to be discovered for many. Some entrepreneurs mistakenly equate efficiency with the mere attainment of goals. They believe that as long as a company fulfills its commitments financially and in terms of customer service, it's competent. However, this perception falls short of reality. In this discussion, we delve into enhancing your company's operational efficiency by highlighting crucial actions and areas of focus.

Operational efficiency refers to the continuous enhancement of all processes that collectively contribute to creating your final product or service. Consider a supermarket as an example. Its internal methods span production, hiring, sales, and communication – all vital cogs that drive the company toward sales targets.

However, hitting sales targets alone doesn't equate to operational efficiency. Imperfect stock control can lead to product spoilage, translating into losses. Significant savings opportunities may slip through the cracks if the procurement department isn't adept at identifying optimal suppliers.

These scenarios emphasize the importance of comprehending your company's intricacies. The core truth is that each venture has its distinct reality regarding processes.

Understanding operational efficiency is pivotal for the longevity and prosperity of your company. It goes beyond surface-level accomplishments and delves into systematically optimizing all operational facets. By perfecting each cog in the intricate machinery of your organization, you reduce wastage, enhance productivity, and uncover potential areas for growth and savings.

Are you on the brink of missing deadlines, struggling to locate essential files, and facing uncertainty about having clean clothes for tomorrow? If this scenario sounds all too familiar, you're not alone.

Disorganization can swiftly consume your time. Those moments spent searching for keys or hunting down emails add significant chunks of lost productivity. Even if you manage to complete tasks, they might not reflect your best efforts. Your capacity to organize tasks and stay on track significantly impacts your success. It ripples through your team and colleagues. Bringing order and tranquility into your routine is a foundation for being productive and a shield against stress.

Maintaining organization at work is an individual responsibility. Relying on your manager or colleagues to organize tasks can strain work relationships. Employers highly value good organizational skills in new hires, and workplaces expect team members to display initiative and professionalism. Being on top of your tasks demonstrates ownership and independence, reducing the need for constant supervision. It's not only a professional trait but also a gesture of respect.

Your organizational efforts benefit your team as well. Adhering to file-naming conventions, for instance, streamlines processes and enhances efficiency for everyone. Punctuality in meetings contributes to their effectiveness.

Even seemingly minor tasks, like keeping shared spaces clutter-free, impact the overall atmosphere and performance in the office. The fundamental rewards of organization and a clutter-free workspace encompass heightened productivity and enhanced performance. This, in turn, cultivates a sense of control, which is crucial for managing stress, building resilience, and fostering well-being.

Organization is a skill, with some naturally more adept than others. Well, anyone can learn and develop organizational abilities. Consistent practice cultivates better organization and the formation of new habits. As a result, you create a conducive, efficient working environment, safeguard your time, and improve communication.[29]

The cornerstone of effective organization lies in establishing robust systems and processes. It's not enough to aim for improvement without a structured plan. The importance of transparent systems and processes becomes evident when considering the analogy of building habits.

Consider the goal of exercising daily. While many aspire to maintain a consistent workout routine, merely desiring this change won't suffice. Individuals can struggle to translate their desires into action without a systematic approach. They lack the scaffolding that systems provide to facilitate their journey. A case in point is the absence of a set schedule, defined process, or a sequence of steps required to integrate daily workouts into their routine seamlessly.

29 https://www.mindtools.com/auj8unv/how-to-be-more-organized

This phenomenon underscores the significance of processes, not just in personal life but across both professional and personal spheres. Attempting to streamline without the backbone of a well-constructed process often leads to inefficiency and frustration. It's akin to having a puzzle without a guiding frame. Systems and processes provide the structure that allows disparate elements to fall together cohesively.

When considering business or work-related endeavors, this principle holds even more weight. Aiming to improve operations, innovate, or boost productivity is admirable, but its realization hinges on establishing an effective process. Without a systematic approach, valuable time and resources may be squandered, and desired outcomes may remain elusive.

The importance of systems and processes cannot be overstated. They form the bedrock upon which habits, efficiency, and productivity are built. Whether in personal aspirations or professional endeavors, having structured processes is the compass that guides intention into tangible achievement.

HARNESSING HABITS AND STRUCTURE FOR SUCCESS

Establishing habits within a structured process is a fundamental strategy underpinning personal growth, professional success, and business productivity. This dynamic interplay between habits and structure forms the basis for consistent achievement and sustainable growth.

Imagine a sales team aiming to boost their performance and exceed targets. While the goal is clear, success is only partially contingent on enthusiasm or isolated efforts. Integrating habits within a structured process ensures team members a more systematic approach to their tasks. For instance, following a well-defined process that includes prospecting, qualifying leads, conducting compelling pitches, and consistent follow-ups creates a roadmap for success. Pairing this structured process with daily goal setting and performance tracking enhances accountability and ensures that each step is executed consistently.

In a business context, operational efficiency thrives when habits are intertwined with structured processes. Consider the example of a manufacturing company seeking to minimize production delays and optimize resource utilization. Implementing a structured process encompassing inventory management, production scheduling, and quality control is crucial. However, regular process audits, identifying bottlenecks, and brainstorming improvement ideas enhance efficiency. This habit-driven approach ensures that the structured process evolves and adapts in real time, reducing waste and improving productivity.

The synergy between habits and structured processes is equally relevant in personal development. For instance, consider the goal of enhancing time management skills. A structured approach involving prioritization, scheduling, and task allocation is a good start. However, the habit of dedicating a few minutes each morning to planning the day and reviewing the progress transforms time management into a sustainable practice.

Integrating habits within a structured process is a potent strategy applied across personal, professional, and business realms. It bridges the gap between intention and action, creating a powerful framework for consistent growth and accomplishment. Individuals and organizations can unlock their full potential by coupling structured processes with purposeful habits, driving progress, productivity, and success.

POWER OF PROCESSES AND SYSTEMS

> *"Systems and processes are the gears that keep the business machinery running smoothly."*
>
> —W. Edwards Deming

RECOGNIZING THE VALUE OF SCHEDULES, PROCESSES, AND SEQUENCES of events is a fundamental pillar in achieving desired outcomes in personal and professional realms. This emphasis underscores the importance of translating aspirations into tangible actions through a well-structured approach.

Consider a marketing campaign as an example. A company envisions launching a successful product campaign to drive sales. While the desire for success is present, the absence of a structured process can lead to missed opportunities. Without a clear schedule outlining tasks, deadlines, and responsibilities, the campaign's execution may lack coordination, resulting in inefficiencies and suboptimal outcomes.

The campaign gains direction by implementing a structured process that includes defining target audiences, crafting compelling content, selecting distribution channels, and setting specific milestones. Each step becomes part of a sequence of events that guides the team toward achieving the desired outcome – a well-executed, impactful marketing campaign.

In a broader organizational context, the significance of schedules, processes, and sequences extends to optimizing resources and achieving greater efficiency. Imagine a manufacturing company aiming to reduce production costs while maintaining product quality. A structured process that includes analyzing resource allocation, streamlining production procedures, and continuous quality checks is essential. By adhering to this process, the company ensures that every aspect of production contributes to the desired outcome of cost-effective, high-quality products. The sequence of events within the process facilitates smooth operations and enables the company to achieve its goals efficiently.

Whether in business or personal endeavors, the synergy between schedules, processes, and sequences empowers individuals and organizations to convert intentions into concrete achievements. By implementing structured processes and adhering to predefined schedules, each step becomes a deliberate action toward success. The deliberate sequence ensures that efforts are well-coordinated and that resources are utilized optimally, leading to the realization of desired outcomes.

STRATEGIC POTENTIAL OF STREAMLINING PROCESSES AND SYSTEMS

Streamlining processes and systems constitutes a strategic approach aimed at dissecting the existing situation, devising a comprehensive plan, and introducing novel ways to enhance operations. It's an endeavor that holds the potential to fortify the efficiency and effectiveness of businesses and organizations across industries.

Imagine your business as a well-orchestrated symphony. Every process or task is a note contributing to a harmonious outcome. However, these notes can sometimes become disjointed, leading to inefficiencies and discord, and streamlining steps to refine these notes ensures that each one flows seamlessly into the next. The concept is intuitive: by identifying areas where processes can be made faster, easier, and more seamless, you pave the way for heightened productivity.

Take a manufacturing company, for instance. By streamlining its production processes, it can minimize bottlenecks, reduce waste, and optimize resource utilization. What once seemed complex and convoluted can be distilled into a precise, efficient sequence of actions. This simplification ensures that tasks are consistently executed, regardless of the person responsible, resulting in smoother operations and improved output quality.

The impact of streamlining is palpable in various domains. Whether shipping products, onboarding new employees, providing healthcare services, or managing financial tasks, the underlying principle remains: create a leaner, more efficient process. Streamlining isn't merely about making things faster; it's about fostering precision and consistency. For instance, streamlining invoicing procedures involves standardizing each step to guarantee uniformity, regardless of who handles the task. This not only accelerates the process but also reduces the likelihood of errors.

Streamlining processes is akin to refining the gears of a well-oiled machine. By optimizing each component, you ensure that the entire mechanism functions cohesively, generating superior results. The quest for streamlining is a commitment to continuous improvement, a journey toward smoother operations, heightened efficiency, and an elevated performance standard.[30]

UNCOVERING AND TACKLING BARRIERS, INEFFICIENCIES, AND BOTTLENECKS

On the journey toward operational excellence and heightened productivity, a pivotal step emerges: identifying and resolving barriers, inefficiencies, and bottlenecks. Like a well-maintained machine, individuals and organizations must frequently appraise and rectify obstacles obstructing advancement.

30 https://www.smartsheet.com/streamlining-processes

Whether termed as barriers, bottlenecks, or inefficiencies, these challenges are inherent to the pursuit of improvement. A tangible illustration of inefficiency lies in the desire to expand knowledge. As the thirst for information grows, the limitation of time becomes increasingly evident.

Imagine dedicating a mere hour daily to enhance understanding or delve into new topics. At first glance, this aspiration might seem untenable, given our hectic schedules. Yet, juxtapose this against the habit of investing three hours in Netflix. By reallocating just one of those hours, the result remains two hours for leisure and an additional hour for personal growth. This example highlights the potential to conquer inefficiencies by pinpointing opportunities to optimize time and effort.

Barriers, akin to roadblocks, are challenges that disrupt the smooth flow of processes. These hurdles encompass outdated practices, inadequate resources, or even resistance to change. The initial move to surmount them is recognition—acknowledging these stumbling blocks empowers organizations to strategize and implement solutions that sidestep or obliterate them.

Inefficiencies, in contrast, signify areas where time, effort, or resources are squandered. These can manifest as excessive steps, avoidable delays, or ineffective resource allocation. Spotting inefficiencies necessitates a discerning evaluation of workflows and actively seeking openings to refine and optimize. Suppose we consider a company manually handling invoices, leading to errors and delays. Noticing this inefficiency, the company might automate the invoicing process, economizing time and reducing errors.

Bottlenecks represent junctures in a process where the flow constricts, breeding delays and stymieing productivity. Spotting bottlenecks mandates meticulous perusal of process flowcharts or real-time scrutiny of operations. Imagine a manufacturing company realizing a specific machine induces delays due to its restricted output capacity. Addressing this bottleneck could enhance overall production speed.

Central to these concepts is the comprehension that the journey toward efficiency and progress is not a singular event but a perpetual cycle characterized by continuous refinement. Progress isn't always about revolutionary leaps; the power of incremental improvements is often underestimated. This notion aligns with the principle of making steady one-percent advancements, consistently progressing toward more outstanding excellence.

Combatting these hindrances mandates a proactive stance, encompassing acknowledgment and formulation and execution of effective remedies. Collaborative endeavors wield considerable influence here. Involving input from team members spanning various organizational tiers can unveil hidden inefficiencies or bottlenecks that might have evaded notice.

Continuous improvement is the north star, propelling organizations and individuals to elevate efficiency consistently. Regular audits and evaluations are imperative to track progress and unearth emerging hindrances. This iterative process facilitates perpetual refinement, guaranteeing solutions remain pertinent and efficacious.

Identifying and surmounting barriers, inefficiencies, and bottlenecks is pivotal for maximizing efficiency and productivity. Through actively pursuing these stumbling blocks, collaborative solution crafting, and embracing the philosophy of unceasing enhancement, entities and individuals lay the groundwork for sustained progress and advancement.

ITERATIVE PATH TO EFFICIENCY AND SUCCESS

The improvement process is inherently iterative, a continuous cycle of refining and advancing toward greater efficiency and effectiveness. This iterative approach is pivotal for individuals and organizations seeking to optimize their productivity and outcomes. Just as each small step forward contributes to a larger stride, the cumulative effect of these incremental improvements propels individuals and businesses closer to their goals.

Within this iterative framework, recurring audits play a critical role. These audits systematically review existing processes and identify bottlenecks, inefficiencies, and barriers hindering progress. By consistently evaluating the efficacy of current practices, individuals and organizations can pinpoint areas that need adjustment or enhancement. These regular assessments act as checkpoints, ensuring that the path of improvement remains aligned with objectives.

Collaboration is another cornerstone of the iterative process. Recognizing that improvement efforts are rarely isolated endeavors, collaboration fosters the exchange of insights and expertise. By involving diverse perspectives, individuals and teams can identify blind spots, generate innovative solutions, and refine strategies collectively. Open communication among team members and stakeholders ensures that improvements are holistic and well-rounded, addressing various aspects of the operation.

Establishing metrics is essential to navigate the journey of enhancement effectively. Metrics provide quantifiable measures of progress and success, offering insights into the impact of implemented changes. These benchmarks serve as a compass, guiding individuals and organizations toward their desired outcomes while fostering accountability.

Simplification emerges as a key theme within this context. The value of streamlining processes and eliminating unnecessary steps cannot be overstated. Uncomplicating processes not only accelerates execution but also reduces the likelihood of errors and bottlenecks. Reducing dependencies, where specific actions must occur before others, empowers smoother workflows and avoids unnecessary delays. By identifying the ideal balance between effort and effectiveness, individuals and organizations can discern when "good enough" is sufficient, avoiding over-complication and inefficiency.

Ultimately, the iterative nature of improvement underscores the importance of consistent effort, regular assessment, and dynamic collaboration. By implementing metrics, simpler processes, and eliminating dependencies, individuals and organizations pave the way for sustainable growth and enhanced productivity.

CREATING STANDARD OPERATING PROCEDURES (SOPS) AND VISUALIZATION BOARDS

In the pursuit of operational excellence, one key aspect is the creation of Standard Operating Procedures (SOPs) and visualization boards. These tools are crucial in transforming abstract concepts into concrete action steps. SOPs are comprehensive documents that outline step-by-step instructions for specific tasks, ensuring consistency and reducing the margin for errors.

These procedures serve as a valuable resource, allowing individuals to follow a predefined path to achieve desired outcomes. They become a reference point for newcomers and seasoned team members, promoting uniformity and clarity in executing tasks. By documenting processes and workflows, organizations establish a robust foundation for efficient operations, minimizing confusion and enhancing overall productivity.

On the other hand, visualization boards offer a visual representation of processes, goals, and objectives. These boards are a tangible reminder of what needs to be achieved and how to get there. Whether it's a physical board in a workspace or a digital tool, visualization boards provide a clear roadmap for individuals to track progress, monitor milestones, and align efforts. These visual cues enhance transparency and accountability, making it easier for teams to stay on course and collaborate effectively. Visualization boards help bridge the gap between conceptual strategies and actionable steps, making them a valuable tool for process optimization.

SHIFT FROM HABIT-BASED ACTIONS TO PROCESS-DRIVEN ACTIONS

The transition from relying solely on individual habits to embracing process-driven actions marks a significant shift in achieving sustainable efficiency and effectiveness. While habits can be powerful, they often lack the structured framework for consistent and scalable success. Conversely, processes provide a systematic approach that incorporates schedules, sequences, and dependencies to yield desired outcomes.

Consider the example of an individual striving to improve their financial situation. They may habitually set aside a small amount of money each month, which is commendable. However, without a well-defined process, this habit might lack direction. The individual transforms their habit into a purposeful action plan by developing a process that outlines specific financial goals, savings targets, and investment strategies. This process-driven approach allows them to systematically track progress, adjust strategies, and work toward achieving financial milestones.

In business, relying solely on individual habits to achieve objectives can lead to inconsistency and reliance on specific individuals. By embracing process-driven actions, organizations establish a structured framework everyone can follow. SOPs ensure that tasks are performed consistently, regardless of the individual executing them. Visualization boards reinforce these processes visually, fostering a culture of clarity and alignment.

The creation of SOPs and visualization boards exemplifies the shift from relying solely on individual habits to adopting process-driven actions. This transition empowers individuals and organizations to operate efficiently, with well-defined steps and visual cues guiding their efforts. By combining the power of processes with visual clarity, businesses can streamline operations, enhance productivity, and achieve sustainable success.

EXCELLENCE OF LEAN METHODOLOGIES

ARE YOU IN THE PURSUIT OF ENHANCING YOUR COMPANY'S PRODUCTIVITY and boosting revenue margins? If so, are you familiar with the concept of lean methodology?

> *"Lean thinking is a way of viewing the whole organization from your customer's perspective."*
>
> —Daniel T. Jones

The concept of lean methodologies has revolutionized the way businesses approach resource management and waste reduction. Rooted in efficiency and continuous improvement principles, lean methodologies provide a framework for organizations to streamline operations, enhance productivity, and eliminate wasteful practices. At its core, lean thinking seeks to maximize value while minimizing waste, improving overall efficiency and customer satisfaction.

One of the fundamental principles of lean methodologies is identifying and eliminating waste, often referred to as "Muda" in the context of lean. Waste can manifest in various forms, such as excess inventory, overproduction, unnecessary movement, defects, waiting times, and underutilized talent. By meticulously analyzing processes and workflows, organizations can identify these waste areas and take proactive measures to eliminate or mitigate them.

Lean methodologies encourage a deep understanding of customer value. This entails defining what the customer truly values and aligning processes to deliver that value while eliminating activities that do not contribute directly to customer satisfaction. This customer-centric approach ensures that resources are allocated to activities that directly enhance the quality of products or services, optimizing resource use.

Lean methodologies also prioritize the involvement and empowerment of frontline employees. These individuals are often closest to the processes and possess valuable insights into areas of improvement. By encouraging employee engagement and collaboration, organizations tap into a wealth of creative solutions that can drive efficiency gains and waste reduction.

CORE PRINCIPLES OF LEAN METHODOLOGY

Are you interested in delving into the core principles of lean methodology? Let's take you through the five foundational principles that underpin this methodology.

VALUE IDENTIFICATION

At the outset of the lean approach, the task is to pinpoint the value that your customers are seeking. This entails understanding the specific problem you're addressing for them and identifying the aspects of your solution that hold value and warrant payment. Any activity or process that doesn't directly contribute to your product or service's value is considered wasteful.

VALUE STREAM MAPPING

Subsequently, it would be best to chart the activities flow within your company to discern areas where value isn't generated. Crafting a value stream map enables a clear view of where value originates and what proportion. This visualization facilitates identifying and eliminating steps that do not contribute value.

SUSTAINING CONTINUOUS WORKFLOW

Having mapped your value stream, it becomes imperative to maintain a consistent and fluid workflow across teams. Process bottlenecks can be promptly spotted and eradicated by breaking down work into smaller units and visualizing the workflow.

IMPLEMENTATION OF A PULL SYSTEM

Establishing a pull system is vital to ensure a stable workflow. This system operates by pulling work only as and when there is a demand for it. This way, resources can be optimized according to capacity, and products or services are delivered only when required.

ONGOING IMPROVEMENT

The final stride involves the continuous enhancement of your lean management system. It's crucial to include employees at all levels in the process of improvement. Practices such as daily stand-up meetings can contribute to daily refinements and process enhancements.[31]

UTILIZING TOOLS AND TECHNIQUES IN LEAN METHODOLOGY

Here are several examples of tools used within the framework of lean methodology:

1. **Kanban:** This technique employs visual boards and Kanban cards to optimize workflows, boost productivity, and reduce wasteful activities in manufacturing and workflow management.

2. **5S:** The 5S methodology involves five sequential steps to optimize workspaces. It aids teams in efficiently organizing their environments by segregating essential tools from non-essential ones, minimizing wasteful practices, and standardizing work procedures.

3. **Kaizen:** Kaizen focuses on continuously enhancing all business functions. Rooted in self-critique, it revolves around five core tenets: teamwork, personal discipline, heightened morale, quality, and suggestions for improvement.

4. **Value Stream Mapping:** This tool visually represents the entire process, from initiation to conclusion. It helps identify and eliminate wasteful elements, enabling businesses to streamline processes and concentrate on activities directly benefiting the customer.

5. **Heijunka:** By enabling manufacturers to balance workloads and produce small batches of varied products, Heijunka reduces inventory and waste.

31 https://chisellabs.com/glossary/what-is-lean-methodology/

6. **Hoshin Kanri:** As a strategic planning tool, Hoshin Kanri aligns business goals with actions, prioritizing critical activities for optimal focus.

7. **Just-In-Time:** This technique produces goods or services exactly when and in the exact quantity required, reducing inventory and minimizing waste.

8. While these lean methodology tools enhance efficiency, they can encounter challenges during implementation due to resistance to change, inconsistent practices, team resistance, lack of engagement, limited management support, and insufficient collaboration and knowledge sharing.

DRIVING EFFICIENCY THROUGH LEAN METHODOLOGY

"The best process is the simplest process. Lean thinking is about simplicity."

—W. Edwards Deming

The story of John D. Rockefeller serves as a compelling example of optimizing processes to achieve greater efficiency and effectiveness. In his pursuit of streamlining operations, Rockefeller faced the challenge of shipping containers of oil, which were stored in drums. The traditional method involved multiple welding points for sealing the lids of these drums. However, through meticulous experimentation and analysis, he sought to determine the optimal number of welding points required to achieve a secure seal.

Rockefeller's dedication to finding the perfect balance between efficiency and effectiveness led him to identify the specific number of welding points necessary for each drum's size. By doing so, he eliminated unnecessary steps, resources, and time without compromising the integrity of the containers. This strategic approach not only reduced waste in the form of excess welding but also streamlined the entire shipping process, from creation to sealing to transportation.

The significance of focusing on value-added activities and eliminating waste becomes evident through this story. By pinpointing and addressing inefficiencies, Rockefeller was able to optimize his shipping process and enhance overall productivity. His example underscores the importance of continually evaluating and refining processes to minimize waste, excess resources, and unnecessary steps.

Embracing value-added activities and shedding processes that do not contribute directly to outcomes allows organizations to channel their efforts and resources toward activities that truly matter. This approach not only enhances efficiency but also drives innovation and progress. By eliminating bottlenecks and barriers, companies can allocate resources effectively and achieve desired outcomes while reducing the strain on the system.

Incorporating lean methodologies, similar to Rockefeller's pursuit of optimal welding points, empowers organizations to systematically identify areas of waste and inefficiency. This involves mapping processes, identifying redundancies, and streamlining activities to maximize output. In essence, the focus shifts from achieving targets to refining the journey toward those targets, ultimately enhancing overall effectiveness and productivity.

The story of John D. Rockefeller underscores the principle that incremental improvements, driven by a commitment to eliminating waste and adding value, profoundly impact an organization's success. By aligning processes with the desired outcomes and adopting a culture of continuous improvement, businesses can position themselves for sustained growth, heightened efficiency, and increased competitiveness.

FROM WASTE REDUCTION TO ONGOING IMPROVEMENT

Pursuing lean methodology and adopting its principles requires a proactive approach to identifying and addressing areas of potential waste at a personal and organizational level. Encouraging individuals within a team or company to recognize and eliminate inefficiencies becomes a cornerstone of this strategy. Like the example of streamlining drum production, wherein excessive weld spots were identified and removed, organizations can benefit from this practice.

Within an organization, the concept is straightforward. If an activity involves 76 steps but only 46 are essential to achieve the objective, then streamlining the process by eliminating the unnecessary 30 steps is paramount. This principle embodies the essence of lean methodology, focusing on value-added tasks and minimizing waste. Encouraging teams to assess their processes and discard redundant or non-essential activities critically aligns with enhancing efficiency.

Implementing new tools and techniques is another crucial facet of adopting lean methodology. These tools are designed to facilitate the identification of inefficiencies and provide structured approaches for addressing them. Processes such as mapping and 5S, which emphasize sorting, setting in order, shining, standardizing, and sustaining, aid in streamlining workflows and reducing efforts. Mapping allows teams to visually represent their processes, making inefficiencies more apparent and enabling targeted improvements. The 5S methodology, on the other hand, contributes to maintaining an organized and efficient workspace by eliminating clutter and standardizing procedures.

Constant vigilance and a commitment to continuous improvement are central to lean methodology. This involves an ongoing process of evaluating and adjusting processes to minimize inefficiencies and maximize output. Organizations that embrace lean principles are dedicated to identifying bottlenecks, redundancies, and inefficiencies as they emerge. They can maintain optimal efficiency by addressing these issues promptly and adjusting processes accordingly.

When embraced and integrated into an organization's culture, lean methodology fosters a proactive attitude toward efficiency. It encourages individuals and teams to constantly seek opportunities for improvement, whether through the elimination of wasteful activities, the adoption of efficient tools, or the ongoing refinement of processes. Through these practices, businesses can minimize waste and enhance productivity, reduce costs, and ultimately achieve higher success in their endeavors.

CREATING A CULTURE OF CONTINUOUS IMPROVEMENT

Instilling a culture of continuous improvement and adaptability within an organization is essential for sustained growth and success. The chapters mentioned highlight the significance of having efficient systems and processes and fostering a mindset of ongoing refinement. This culture encourages individuals and teams to identify inefficiencies, overcome obstacles, and embrace change, enhancing productivity and effectiveness.

Continuous improvement recognizes that there's always room for enhancement, even inefficient processes. This mindset promotes a proactive approach to problem-solving, encouraging employees to seek out areas for optimization. It's not merely about achieving goals but consistently seeking ways to surpass them.

Adaptability is equally crucial in this framework. With the ever-evolving business landscape, organizations that can swiftly respond to change and pivot their strategies will likely thrive. A culture that values adaptability empowers employees to be open to new ideas, experiment with innovative approaches, and seamlessly transition when circumstances require it.

This culture of continuous improvement and adaptability begins at the top. Leaders should model these behaviors, encouraging their teams to think critically, experiment with new methods, and embrace change without fear. Open communication channels provide a platform for sharing insights, soliciting feedback, and brainstorming solutions collaboratively.

One practical example within this context is the concept of lean methodologies. Similar to the story of John D. Rockefeller streamlining the shipping of oil containers, organizations can identify and eliminate areas of waste and inefficiency. By fostering a culture where all team members actively seek these opportunities, the organization becomes agile and better equipped to respond to challenges.

Acknowledging the significance of ongoing learning and development contributes to this culture. Encouraging employees to enhance their skills and knowledge continuously fosters a competent and innovative workforce. Providing training and resources to support this development reinforces the commitment to improvement.

Creating a continuous improvement and adaptability culture is not just about implementing processes; it's about nurturing a mindset that values refinement, experimentation, and staying open to change. This culture propels organizations forward, equipping them to navigate challenges, optimize processes, and embrace growth opportunities.[32]

CULTIVATING A CULTURE OF NEVER-ENDING DEVELOPMENT

In the pursuit of organizational excellence, establishing an unbroken feedback cycle emerges as pivotal. This cycle doesn't solely encompass team members but extends its reach to each individual, recognizing that progress thrives on collective endeavor and personal dedication. Anchored in this strategy is the strategic use of metrics and decisions founded on data, which act as unwavering beacons illuminating the advancement journey. Through dissecting these metrics, it's possible to spot trends and potential concerns, allowing for timely course corrections and adept task prioritization.

A cornerstone of fostering an environment of perpetual betterment is actively enlisting participation from all corners of the organization. This participation isn't confined to professional domains; it permeates the fabric of camaraderie within teams. These principles echo through history, from the Army's call to be an "army of one" to the Marines' rallying cry to "adapt and overcome." Such principles, tried and tested, encapsulate the essence of ceaseless refinement and adaptability.

They sculpt a culture of continuous improvement and adaptability, fueling team members' innate sense of ownership and accountability. Empowering them to partake in decision-making deepens their engagement and intensifies their dedication to the organization's objectives. At its heart, this approach thrives on transparent communication, embracing feedback as an indispensable instrument for growth. When individuals witness their

32 https://blog.kainexus.com/continuous-improvement/culture-of-continuous-improvement/7-surefire-ways-to-promote-continuous-improvement-in-the-workplace

opinions being heard and transformed into action, their investment in the organization's triumph swells organically.

Fundamentally, this culture pivots on empowerment. Team members are encouraged to embrace their work with ownership, shouldering responsibility for the outcomes they contribute. This sense of accountability propels them to actively search for avenues of enhancement, question established norms, and contribute dynamically to the organization's overall efficacy.

The embedding of feedback cycles, the infusion of metrics and decisions rooted in data, and the nurturing of a culture of unceasing advancement all weave together to fashion an ecosystem where progress isn't an isolated destination but a continuous expedition. Organizations lay down the tracks for evolution, expansion, and unwavering allegiance to excellence through invigorating participation, bestowing empowerment, and fostering forthright communication.

EMPOWERING GROWTH THROUGH TRAINING AND DEVELOPMENT

> *"The greatest asset of a company is its people. Investing in their growth through training is an investment in the company's success."*
>
> —Richard Branson

A cornerstone of fostering a culture of continuous improvement lies in the notion of ownership and responsibility among team members. Achieving this involves a fundamental shift toward involving them in decision-making processes. Within this context, open communication becomes a linchpin, as does the art of soliciting feedback. Empowering individuals to take ownership of their work catalyzes enhanced efficiency across the organization.

This holistic approach acknowledges that the collective is greater than the sum of its parts.

Crucially, this journey toward growth encompasses providing opportunities for individual and organizational development. This includes the essential aspect of training – a mechanism that hones existing skills and introduces new ones. An insightful observation highlights that around 68% of employees favor on-the-job learning, and an even higher percentage (59%) acknowledges the tangible benefits of training in improving overall performance.

Delving deeper into this concept, it's evident that organizations embracing a strong learning culture stand to reap significant rewards. Employees who remain invested in their personal and professional growth often find themselves more committed to the organization's mission. Such dedication results in a notable retention rate increase of 30% to 50%, a powerful indicator of an environment that values individual development.

Contrastingly, neglecting training and skill development can lead to an alarming 40% of employees departing from their positions within a year. To avert such turnover, it becomes imperative for organizations to champion learning. Recognizing achievements and delivering performance-based rewards further reinforce the loop of motivation and progress.

The process encapsulates a symbiotic relationship: providing tools and resources to foster growth and, in turn, nurturing an environment of continuous improvement. This harmonious cycle reverberates throughout the organization, resulting in engaged, empowered employees who contribute wholeheartedly to its success. Thus, the strategic investment in training and skill development lays the groundwork for a vibrant growth, development, and innovation ecosystem.

UTILIZING AUTOMATION AND TECHNOLOGY

"The future is digital. There is no doubt about that."
—Marissa Mayer

TECHNOLOGY'S ROLE IN THE DYNAMIC REALM OF BUSINESS HAS transcended convenience to become a driving force for efficiency. This transition is exemplified by the journey from reliance on physical planning books to the present era, where automation is the bedrock of process refinement.

The shift toward automation has reshaped task management, optimization, and execution. While physical planning books may have sufficed in the past, today's intricate business landscape demands more sophisticated solutions. Adopting automation transforms from a mere choice into a strategic necessity as technology evolves.

Elevating efficiency through technology entails a strategic progression. Firstly, it mandates a proactive approach to recognize, evaluate, and select technology solutions that align with organizational objectives. This calls for meticulous evaluation, gauging compatibility, and forecasting the potential impact on productivity.

The subsequent pivotal stage involves seamlessly integrating technology into existing workflows. Here, technology ceases to be a standalone tool, morphing into an intrinsic part of how work unfolds. Successful integration necessitates the harmonious coalescence of technological tools and human processes.

However, the journey isn't complete at integration. Ensuring technology's successful assimilation among team members entails a strategic focus on training and support. Transitioning from traditional methods to technology-driven paradigms can involve a learning curve. To alleviate this, organizations must invest in comprehensive training initiatives and ongoing support to ensure seamless utilization.

By harnessing technology and automation, organizations unlock an array of advantages. Repetitive and time-consuming tasks are automated, allowing team members to focus on strategic and value-driven pursuits. This not only optimizes productivity but also resource allocation. Furthermore, technology empowers data-guided decision-making by furnishing valuable insights through metrics and analysis.

The shift toward technology and automation marks a fundamental reimagination of organizational functioning. From simplifying workflows to propelling data-driven strategies, technology presents an avenue to achieve unparalleled efficiency. The essence lies in strategically identifying, incorporating, and adapting these solutions, ultimately forging the path toward a more streamlined and agile organization.

LEVERAGING TECHNOLOGY FOR ENHANCED EFFICIENCY

In the quest for operational excellence, the strategic incorporation of technology takes the spotlight. As organizations strive to refine their processes, technology emerges as a potent catalyst for amplifying communication, streamlining data management, and uncovering avenues for heightened efficiency and effectiveness.

Let's discuss significant areas where technology and automation will elevate productivity and efficiency records.

1. EMPOWERING COMMUNICATION THROUGH TECHNOLOGY

Effective communication is the linchpin of operational success in today's dynamic business environment. Technology emerges as the catalyst that fuels seamless and instantaneous communication within organizations. From digital platforms to collaborative software and communication apps, these tools dismantle barriers and enable teams to share information, updates, and insights effortlessly. By capitalizing on technology, organizations transcend geographical limitations, ensuring that vital information reaches the right stakeholders in real time.

2. EFFICIENT DATA MANAGEMENT

Data stands as a potent driver of decision-making and strategic planning. Here, technology takes center stage in data management, automating vast data-sets collection, storage, and analysis. This data-driven approach empowers organizations to make informed choices, track key performance indicators, and spot trends that steer future strategies. Digital solutions uphold data precision, accessibility, and security, amplifying operational effectiveness.

3. UNSHACKLING FROM REPETITIVE TASKS

Automation emerges as a game-changer when shedding the weight of repetitive and time-consuming tasks. By automating routine processes, organizations optimize resource allocation and mitigate human error. This newfound efficiency allows employees to shift focus from manual tasks to more strategic pursuits, necessitating critical thinking, innovation, and creative problem-solving. Consequently, organizations witness heightened productivity and an expanded capacity for ingenuity.

4. CRAFTING AUTOMATION SOLUTIONS

The seamless integration of automation solutions calls for a systematic approach. Organizations must discern tasks primed for automation and harmoniously meld technology into established workflows. Initial deployment is the starting point; sustained evaluation and refinement are crucial. Regular assessments unearth opportunities for further automation, optimization, and enhancement. An adaptable stance toward automation ensures the organization remains agile, adeptly responding to evolving business demands.

5. NAVIGATING TOMORROW WITH EMERGING TECHNOLOGIES

The technological terrain races forward, compelling organizations to stay in sync with emergent trends to uphold competitiveness. A prime example is the advent of Artificial Intelligence (AI). AI's capability to emulate human intelligence and decision-making is a potential revolutionizer. For instance, AI-driven chatbots can deftly handle customer queries, freeing human agents for intricate interactions. Machine learning algorithms decode data patterns, predicting market trends and consumer behavior to inform strategic decisions.

6. RESHAPING FORCE OF AI

Artificial Intelligence, as a budding technology, holds the sway to reshape industries across the board. AI algorithms dissect colossal datasets via machine learning to unearth insights that may elude human perception. AI algorithms scrutinize medical images to pinpoint anomalies in healthcare, propelling early disease detection. In manufacturing, AI-fueled predictive maintenance forestalls downtime by preempting equipment failures. By harnessing AI's potency, organizations unlock an unprecedented realm of efficiency and effectiveness.

The expedition toward operational brilliance is intricately intertwined with technology's sway. Technology bolsters communication expedites data management, liberates resources, and unfurls avenues for innovation. Integrating automation solutions calls for prudent planning and ceaseless evaluation to optimize outcomes. Furthermore, vigilance toward burgeoning technologies like AI proves pivotal in unearthing novel dimensions of efficiency and effectiveness. As organizations embrace technology's transformative potential, they position themselves to thrive in an ever-shifting business panorama.

CONCLUSION

In the dynamic realm of modern business, the quest for excellence remains a perpetual voyage fueled by the engines of efficiency, innovation, and adaptability. Throughout this exploration, we've traversed the intricate landscape of heightened productivity and effectiveness, unveiling the power of well-structured systems, the significance of fostering a culture of perpetual advancement, and the transformative potential of harnessing technology.

From the outset, the spotlight shone on the pivotal role of systems and processes in propelling productivity. We've delved deep into cultivating structured habits' profound impact and recognized how schedules and sequences steer us toward our desired destinations. The art of process refinement emerged, illuminating a path marked by iterative progress, waste reduction, and the crafting of standardized procedures. At the same time, lean methodologies wove a compelling narrative, shedding light on the intricate dance between value creation and the eradication of inefficiencies—a journey elegantly epitomized by the saga of John D. Rockefeller.

Yet, the narrative didn't stop at operational efficacy alone. The canvas expanded to encapsulate the crucial domain of nurturing a culture of unwavering advancement. Masterstrokes on this canvas were the journey into decision-making involvement, the vitality of feedback loops, and the empowerment bestowed through training and resource allocation. The revelation resonated beyond corporate confines, painting a picture that extended to personal growth, societal elevation, and the never-ending quest for advancement.

As we integrated technology and automation, a realm of boundless horizons materialized. The symphony of enriched communication, streamlined data orchestration, and liberation from repetitive tasks orchestrated by automation played to the tune of progress. The symphony crescendo with the resounding call to be vigilant of technological strides. Here, the transformative cadence of Artificial Intelligence (AI) stood tall, poised to reshape industries and redefine possibilities.

In the grand finale, the chapter harmonized the essence of efficient systems, relentless betterment, and technological prowess. It encapsulated the spirit of fostering an ecosystem where innovation thrives, change is embraced, and individuals and organizations ascend to zeniths of achievement. As the curtain descends on this chapter, the journey to excellence continues—nurtured by structured systems, enriched by a culture of perpetual learning, and propelled by the dynamic might of technology. This journey is crafted upon the loom of progress, weaving threads of evolution and endurance in the relentless pursuit of perfection.

IMPORTANCE OF BEING ORGANIZED

"Organization isn't a luxury; it's a strategy to help you achieve your goals and live your best life."

—Lori Greiner

PART 5

MAKING A GLOBAL IMPACT

CHAPTER TEN

ENVIRONMENTAL SUSTAINABILITY

When stressed or disconnected, many of us instinctively seek solace in nature, taking walks in forests, parks, beaches, or along country roads. This natural inclination reflects the profound connection between human well-being and environmental health. Approximately 24% of global human fatalities can be attributed, either directly or indirectly, to avoidable environmental factors.

To lead long and healthy lives, we require and deserve clean air to breathe, pure water to drink, and toxin-free living spaces.

"The greatest threat to our planet is the belief that someone else will save it."

—Robert Swan

Individuals are the linchpin in the urgent pursuit of environmental sustainability. Within the daunting global environmental challenges, it's crucial to acknowledge that collective efforts begin on an individual level. Each person possesses the potential to wield significant influence for positive change by adopting sustainable practices and thoughtful choices in daily life.

The role of individuals in advancing environmental sustainability cannot be emphasized enough. Their actions, no matter how seemingly small, collectively shape our planet's future. From reducing carbon footprints through energy-efficient living to advocating for eco-friendly policies and supporting sustainable products and industries, individuals can initiate a ripple effect beyond their immediate influence. Let's explore how individuals can contribute to and propel the essential movement toward a more sustainable and harmonious coexistence with the environment.

WASTE REDUCTION

In a world where environmental concerns are rising, each person wields the power to be an active catalyst for change. Through conscious choices and daily routines, individuals can play a pivotal role in preserving the well-being of our planet. One of the most accessible and impactful ways to do so is by focusing on waste reduction. This encompasses efforts to minimize waste generation, responsible disposal practices, and adopting behaviors promoting sustainable resource use.

Reducing waste involves conscious efforts and practices to decrease the volume of materials that harm the environment in landfills. It means minimizing waste creation, seeking sustainable materials management, and prioritizing resource efficiency and environmental stewardship.

Critical components of waste reduction encompass the following:

Prevention: The primary aim is to prevent waste generation, achieved by making mindful choices like buying minimally packaged products, opting for durable items, and reducing overconsumption.

Reuse: Waste reduction also entails reusing items instead of discarding them, whether through repurposing, repairing, or choosing reusable alternatives to disposables.

Recycling: Recycling converts waste materials into new products, lowering the environmental impact of production by reducing the need for new resources. Proper sorting and disposal of recyclables are vital.

Composting: Organic waste like food scraps and yard debris can be transformed into nutrient-rich soil amendments through composting, diverting organic waste from landfills and enhancing soil quality.

Eco-friendly Purchasing: Informed shopping choices involve selecting products made from recyclable or biodegradable materials, supporting sustainable businesses, and avoiding single-use items.

Waste Reduction in Manufacturing: Larger-scale waste reduction comes from efficient manufacturing processes that minimize material waste and energy consumption.

Reducing waste calls for a holistic approach to consumption and resource management, encouraging individuals, businesses, and communities to rethink habits and practices to minimize environmental impact. Doing so, we conserve resources, mitigate pollution, lower greenhouse gas emissions, and contribute to the planet's well-being.

COMMON PRACTICES THAT REDUCE WASTE

Every day, we unintentionally do things that directly or indirectly contribute to catalyzing the waste production process. We make a few tiny and common mistakes that destroy our environment. Keep in mind that it takes nothing but a little effort. Just paying attention to our trivial, regular actions could trigger change. So, let's discuss some practical eco-friendly tips that can have a lasting positive impact on the environment:

Opt for Reusable Containers for On-the-Go Drinks: Instead of using single-use cups and bottles, consider using a reusable water bottle or cup when you're out and about. If you already have a reusable bottle, make it a routine to use it consistently. This not only saves you money but also lessens waste. Carrying your drink discourages spontaneous purchases of costly single-use beverages, reducing the need for disposable containers. Notably, the production and transportation of cans and bottles consume significant energy resources.

Utilize Reusable Grocery Bags Beyond Shopping: Expand the utility of your reusable grocery bags to purposes beyond grocery shopping. If you often forget them, try jotting down a reminder at the top of your grocery list or keep the bags readily accessible in your car's rear seat. Some grocery stores even offer a small refund, typically around 5 cents per reusable bag, which not only saves you a few cents but also curtails the usage of disposable plastic bags.

Make Informed Purchases and Recycle: When shopping, choose products with minimal packaging and opt for items that come in recyclable materials. Awareness of which plastics are recyclable in your area is crucial, as not all plastics are accepted everywhere. Check the recycling codes on labels (e.g., 1 and 2 are commonly accepted) to make eco-conscious choices. Proper recycling ensures that materials are processed efficiently, reducing the demand for virgin resources.

Embrace Composting: Up to a quarter of the items in your trash can be composted, including fruit and vegetable scraps, coffee grounds, eggshells, and yard waste. Composting, although requiring some effort, offers valuable rewards. It diverts organic waste from landfills and provides nutrient-rich soil for gardening. Composting reduces the volume of waste sent to landfill sites and naturally enriches your garden soil.

Avoid Single-Use Containers and Utensils: Avoid single-use food and drink containers, disposable utensils, straws, and napkins whenever possible. Some establishments offer discounts for bringing your reusable mug or containers, so keep them handy. Also, consider supporting reusable silverware, plates, bowls, and cups at work to reduce disposable waste during lunch breaks. Adopting these habits will help reduce the demand for single-use items and minimize the waste entering landfills.

Buy Secondhand and Donate Used Goods: Consider the eco-conscious choice of buying secondhand before purchasing new items. This approach saves you money, supports local charities, and prevents things from ending in landfills. Explore thrift stores like Goodwill for secondhand clothes, visit places like Habitat for Humanity's ReStore for used furniture and repurposed construction materials, or search platforms like Craigslist for budget-friendly deals on various items, such as bicycles. Choosing secondhand helps you find unique items and contributes to a more sustainable and environmentally friendly consumption pattern.

Remember, donating items you no longer need or use extends their lifespan and reduces waste. This practice promotes a circular economy where goods are reused and repurposed instead of discarded.

Shop Local Farmers Markets and Buy in Bulk: Shopping at your local farmers market provides numerous benefits. Not only do you support local farmers and promote regional agriculture, but you also gain access to fresher ingredients than in supermarkets. Locally produced food typically requires shorter transportation distances and less refrigeration, reducing the carbon footprint associated with food distribution. Many local farmers embrace minimal packaging practices, and some even welcome the return of items like berry baskets or egg cartons for reuse. To further reduce packaging waste, consider shopping at stores offering bulk food. However, be prepared and bring your reusable containers along to minimize packaging waste.

Curb Your Use of Paper: Mail, Receipts, Magazines: In today's digital age, many companies offer the option to receive bills and statements by email, and some incentivize this eco-friendly choice. Similarly, more stores offer electronic receipts (e-receipts), which are environmentally friendly and more challenging to misplace if you need to return an item. Consider subscribing to digital versions of your favorite magazines, which you can read on your tablet or computer. Digital subscriptions often come at a lower cost than their hard-copy counterparts, significantly reducing the demand for paper production and distribution.

By incorporating these practices into your lifestyle, you can reduce packaging waste, minimize your carbon footprint, and conserve valuable resources while enjoying the benefits of fresher, locally sourced products and a more organized, paperless approach to daily tasks. These small changes add up to substantially and positively impact the environment.[33]

CONSERVING RESOURCES

Conserving resources involves the responsible and sustainable utilization of natural materials, energy, and other assets to meet current needs while safeguarding the ability of future generations to meet their own needs. This practice centers on waste reduction, efficient resource utilization, and exploring low-impact alternatives. The significance of resource conservation cannot be overstated, and here are key rationales for its critical importance:

Environmental Safeguarding: Resource conservation serves as a shield for the environment by curtailing the extraction of raw materials, minimizing pollution, and reducing greenhouse gas emissions linked to resource acquisition and processing. This helps counter habitat destruction, deforestation, and other environmental harm.

Sustainable Legacy: By conserving resources today, we guarantee an adequate supply for future generations. Resource depletion can trigger scarcities, price volatility, and conflicts over access, all of which can negatively affect the prospects of future populations.

Energy Efficiency: Resource conservation typically dovetails with heightened energy efficiency. The judicious utilization of resources reduces energy waste during extraction, processing, and transport. Consequently, this results in diminished energy consumption, lowered greenhouse gas emissions, and reduced energy expenses.

33 https://www.nature.org/en-us/about-us/where-we-work/united-states/delaware/stories-in-delaware/delaware-eight-ways-to-reduce-waste/

Economic Gains: Resource conservation can offer economic benefits. Enterprises that optimize resource utilization often reduce operational expenditures, bolster their financial performance, and enhance competitiveness. Furthermore, advancing sustainable technologies and practices can spawn fresh economic openings and job prospects.

Biodiversity Protection: Many resources are intricately linked to ecosystems, and their overexploitation can induce biodiversity loss and ecosystem deterioration. Resource conservation aids in the preservation of habitats and fosters the flourishing of species, contributing to overall biodiversity preservation.

Climate Change Mitigation: Resource conservation is pivotal in mitigating climate change. By trimming greenhouse gas emissions linked to resource acquisition and consumption, we contribute to global endeavors to restrict temperature escalation and its associated consequences.

Resilience: An approach to resource use rooted in sustainability heightens the resilience of communities and ecosystems. Relying on renewable resources and conducting responsible management better equips us to contend with environmental fluctuations and adversities.

Environmental Equity: Resource conservation can foster environmental equity by ensuring that all communities partake in the benefits of resource utilization while diminishing detrimental consequences. Sustainable practices can alleviate environmental disparities and irregularities in resource availability.

Conserving resources is a fundamental tenet of environmental sustainability and conscientious guardianship of our planet. It safeguards the environment and secures a more equitable and prosperous future for all. By acknowledging the significance of resource conservation and adopting sustainable approaches, we can shield our planet's ecosystems, conserve invaluable resources, and mold a more robust and sustainable world.

HOW TO CONSERVE RESOURCES

Resource conservation is a shared responsibility that extends to individuals worldwide. Our daily actions wield substantial influence in a world grappling with escalating environmental challenges. Resource preservation is not solely the domain of experts or large organizations; it commences with each of us within our households, workplaces, and communities. It involves a voyage marked by conscious decisions and sustainable behaviors, actions that lessen our impact on the planet and contribute to an egalitarian and resilient future.

Let's delve into pragmatic approaches and tactics individuals can effortlessly integrate into their lives. These steps aim to conserve resources, curtail waste, and fulfill a pivotal role in safeguarding the environment for posterity.

Practice Recycling: Recycling is a foundational resource conservation practice. It involves collecting and processing materials like paper, glass, plastic, and metal to create new products. Individuals can participate by sorting recyclables, following local recycling guidelines, and ensuring clean and contaminants-free items.

Use Energy-Efficient Lighting: Transitioning to energy-efficient lighting options, such as LED or CFL bulbs, can significantly reduce energy consumption. These bulbs have longer lifespans and lower electricity usage, leading to reduced energy bills and a smaller environmental footprint.

Opt for Reusable Items: Choose reusable products over disposable ones whenever possible. Examples include reusable water bottles, coffee cups, and shopping bags. This practice minimizes waste and conserves resources used to produce single-use items.

Conserve Water: Water conservation is crucial, especially in water scarcity regions. Individuals can save water by turning off faucets while brushing their teeth, fixing leaky taps, and using water-saving appliances like low-flow showerheads and toilets.

Reduce Energy Consumption at Home: Lower your home's energy consumption by sealing drafts, improving insulation, and setting thermostats to energy-efficient temperatures. Unplug electronics when not in use, and consider installing solar panels or using renewable energy sources.

Embrace Sustainable Transportation: Reduce personal vehicle usage to decrease fossil fuel consumption and air pollution. Whenever possible, walk or bike for short trips, and consider carpooling or using public transportation for longer journeys.

Be Mindful of Packaging: Make informed purchases by avoiding products with excessive or non-recyclable packaging. Choose items with minimal or recyclable packaging materials.

Utilize Renewable Energy: If available, switch to renewable energy sources such as solar or wind power for your home. Many regions offer incentives and programs to support this transition.

Thrift Shopping: Purchase secondhand items from thrift stores to reduce the demand for new products, conserving resources. Thrifting also supports a circular economy, promoting the reuse and repurposing of goods.

Go Paperless: Reduce paper consumption by embracing digital solutions whenever possible. Opt for electronic billing, digital note-taking, and e-books to minimize paper usage.

Embrace Minimalism: Adopt a minimalist lifestyle by reducing the number of possessions and prioritizing quality over quantity. This reduces resource consumption, less waste, and a simpler, more sustainable lifestyle.

Reduce Meat Consumption: Cutting back on meat consumption, especially red meat, can lower the environmental impact associated with livestock farming. Plant-based diets require fewer resources and produce fewer greenhouse gas emissions.

Segregate Waste: Proper waste segregation at home ensures that recyclables, compostable materials, and non-recyclables are disposed of separately. This practice facilitates more efficient recycling and composting processes.

By adopting these practices and making them a part of your daily life, you can play a significant role in conserving resources, reducing waste, and promoting a more sustainable future for our planet. Small individual actions can substantially and positively impact resource conservation and environmental preservation when multiplied.[34]

JOURNEY OF SUSTAINABLE TRANSFORMATION

> *"Sustainability is no longer about doing less harm. It's about doing more good."*
>
> —Jochen Zeitz

THE PRACTICES OF REDUCING WASTE AND CONSERVING RESOURCES embody a holistic and all-encompassing approach to personal consumption and sustainability. These endeavors revolve around

34 https://rightsofnature.org.ph/ways-to-conserve-natural-resources/

the profound realization that individuals can scrutinize their consumption patterns, enact purposeful alterations, and perpetually evaluate their influence on the environment.

At its core, reducing waste signifies a departure from the conventional "use and dispose" mentality toward a more conscientious and deliberate approach to consumption. This approach involves meticulously dissecting daily routines, assessing habits, and pinpointing areas where materials and resources are squandered. Whether it's excess packaging, single-use items, or energy inefficiencies, identifying these wasteful practices is the initial step toward curbing unnecessary resource depletion.

Conserving resources entails an astute recognition of the finite nature of our planet's natural assets. It encompasses the prudent management of energy, water, raw materials, and other essential elements to ensure sustainable availability for current and future generations. Individuals become upholders of these invaluable resources by embracing energy-efficient technologies, reducing water waste, and favoring responsible sourcing.

These sustainable practices, rooted in a thorough analysis of personal consumption patterns, go beyond mere awareness. They necessitate purposeful change. Individuals embark on a transformative journey where they actively participate in creating a more eco-conscious lifestyle. Energy-efficient appliances, reusable products, and responsible waste management become the new norm, replacing outdated, wasteful habits.

However, the process doesn't end with the initial adoption of sustainable practices; it thrives on continuous self-assessment and improvement. Regular evaluations allow individuals to gauge their progress, refine their approaches, and explore additional ways to minimize their environmental footprint. Sustainability becomes an evolving endeavor characterized by adaptability and innovation.

Let's look at reducing waste, conserving resources, and integrating sustainable materials more narratively.

PROCESS OF ADOPTING SUSTAINABLE LIFESTYLE

In mounting environmental challenges, embarking on a sustainability journey has never been more crucial. It begins with critically examining our daily lives, meticulously analyzing how we consume resources and a profound commitment to reducing waste. Here's a description of how this transformation unfolds:

1. **Self-Reflection and Consumption Patterns:** The journey commences with self-reflection. It's about looking inward, examining our habits, and acknowledging our role in resource consumption and waste generation. This moment of introspection lays the foundation for change. We scrutinize our energy consumption, water usage and even dissect our trash to understand where inefficiencies lurk.

2. **Setting the Clear Objectives:** With newfound clarity, we set objectives - specific, measurable, and time-bound. These are not vague aspirations but precise targets. We might resolve to reduce our carbon footprint by using 10% less energy in the next year or eliminating waste by perfecting our recycling and composting routines. These objectives serve as our guiding stars.

3. **Art of Implementation:** Change doesn't occur by wishful thinking alone. It's about action, about implementing meaningful changes in our lives. For energy

conservation, we might embrace energy-efficient appliances and adopt habits like turning off lights when we leave a room. To reduce waste, we shun single-use plastics, establish a seamless recycling system, and introduce composting to give organic waste a second life. These changes require effort and determination.

4. **Creating Sustainable Systems:** To ensure the longevity of our efforts, we build systems and programs within our homes. We construct organized recycling stations with bins for each material, simplifying the recycling process. Timers, sensors, and smart devices manage our energy consumption intelligently. Composting systems take root in our backyards, or we participate in community composting programs.

5. **Habit Formation:** Habits become our allies. They transform us. Turning off lights becomes second nature; recycling is no longer a chore but an instinct. We enjoy composting, watching organic waste turn into rich, nutrient-filled soil. Habits are the unsung heroes of sustainability, quietly guiding our actions.

6. **Sustaining the Momentum:** Sustainability is an unceasing journey. We regularly assess our strategies, measuring progress against our objectives. We look for gaps, for areas where we can enhance our efforts. Staying informed about emerging eco-friendly technologies and practices allows us to adapt and fine-tune our approach.

7. **Integrating Sustainability:** Then there's the matter of the materials we bring into our lives. We seek out products with sustainability certifications, from Energy Star appliances that reduce energy consumption to

FSC-certified wood products that safeguard forests. We choose items crafted from recycled materials, completing the circle of responsible consumption.

This comprehensive approach, grounded in self-awareness and fueled by action, empowers us to champion sustainability in our daily lives. It's not a mere alteration of habits; it's a lifestyle transformation. It's a commitment to reducing waste, conserving precious resources, and embracing sustainable materials, aiming to foster a more responsible and conscious way of living. In this journey, each individual becomes a keeper of the planet, leaving a legacy of positive environmental change for generations.

Reducing waste and conserving resources empowers individuals to redefine their relationship with the environment. It signifies a shift from passive consumers to proactive keepers of the planet. By acknowledging the profound impact of personal choices and embracing the responsibility of sustainable living, individuals contribute to a brighter, more harmonious future where the needs of both humanity and Earth are in harmony.

FOSTERING SUSTAINABILITY THROUGH SUPPORT

The quest for sustainability extends beyond individual actions to endorsing environmentally conscious initiatives and businesses. It hinges on the understanding that personal consumption represents just one facet of the equation; the other aspect entails engaging with organizations and endeavors that share a deep commitment to environmental responsibility and conscious practices.

BACKING ECO-CONSCIOUS ENTERPRISES

Backing eco-conscious enterprises is a pivotal method in the drive to champion environmental awareness and foster sustainability within today's dynamic marketplace. Making the deliberate choice to align with businesses that steadfastly prioritize sustainable values holds the potential to reverberate with far-reaching positive impacts on our planet and society.

1. ETHICAL SOURCING

Eco-conscious enterprises place a robust emphasis on the practice of ethical sourcing. This signifies their unwavering commitment to acquiring materials and ingredients through processes that inflict minimal environmental harm and respect fundamental human rights. Consider, for instance, businesses sourcing fair-trade coffee beans or using sustainably harvested wood in their product lines. When consumers opt to patronize such businesses, they actively participate in reducing the adverse social and environmental consequences entwined with irresponsible sourcing.

2. WASTE MINIMIZATION

A multitude of eco-friendly companies spearhead waste reduction endeavors. They continuously seek inventive approaches to curtail waste throughout their production cycles and packaging methods. These initiatives encompass the utilization of recycled materials, the creation of products designed for extended lifespans, and the implementation of streamlined recycling programs. When consumers make purchases from these enterprises, they indirectly endorse the concept of a circular economy, where resources are employed more efficiently, and the volume of waste destined for landfills is diminished.

3. MINIMIZED CARBON FOOTPRINT

Green enterprises consistently prioritize the mitigation of their carbon footprint. This includes investments in clean energy sources, optimization of transportation logistics, and integration of energy-efficient technologies. By supporting such initiatives, consumers play an active role in the collective battle against climate change and the widespread adoption of sustainable energy practices within the business sphere.

4. DIVERSE ECO-CONSCIOUS PRODUCTS AND SERVICES

The contemporary landscape abounds with a diverse array of eco-conscious products and services. Sustainable fashion labels proffer clothing crafted from organic and recycled materials. Ethically sourced foods and beverages grant consumers access to choices harmonizing with their principles. Green energy providers supply renewable energy solutions, while enterprises specializing in eco-friendly household items offer alternatives to single-use plastics and other ecologically detrimental products. This rich diversity empowers consumers to weave sustainable choices into various facets of their daily lives.

5. CONSUMER DEMAND AND INDUSTRY GROWTH

When individuals proactively opt for eco-conscious products and services, they transmit an unambiguous message to the market that sustainability ranks high on their agenda. This burgeoning consumer demand galvanizes established businesses to embrace more eco-friendly practices and kindles the growth of novel eco-conscious enterprises. As these ventures thrive, they become more accessible to a broader audience, democratizing sustainable products and services and rendering them increasingly mainstream and cost-effective.

Supporting eco-conscious enterprises is a potent conduit through which individuals can leave an indelible positive imprint on the environment and society. It impels ethical sourcing, waste reduction, and carbon footprint mitigation while propelling the expansion of environmentally aware industries. Consumers emerge as torchbearers of environmental consciousness within the contemporary marketplace by consciously aligning with businesses firmly rooted in sustainable values.

MOMENTUM OF COLLECTIVE ACTION

The power of supporting eco-friendly initiatives and businesses lies in the collective momentum it generates, transcending individual decisions and paving the way for a more sustainable future. This collective action represents a force for genuine change on a larger scale.

UNIFIED COMMITMENT

A unified commitment to sustainability emerges when consumers, businesses, and initiatives align in their dedication to environmental stewardship. This collective commitment goes beyond individual efforts and creates a shared vision for a greener, more responsible future.

AMPLIFIED IMPACT

Collective action amplifies the impact of individual choices. As more people and organizations embrace eco-friendly practices and products, the demand for sustainable alternatives grows. This, in turn, encourages businesses to adopt more environmentally friendly practices and innovate in sustainable technologies and products.

CULTURAL SHIFT

A collective dedication to sustainability can lead to a cultural shift where eco-consciousness becomes the norm rather than the exception. It promotes a culture of mindfulness about the environment, where individuals are more likely to consider the environmental impact of their actions and purchases.

ECONOMIC INFLUENCE

The collective support for eco-friendly businesses and initiatives sends a clear economic message. It demonstrates that sustainability is not just a trend but a fundamental value, influencing market trends and business strategies. This can lead to the development of new, sustainable industries and job opportunities.

GLOBAL IMPACT

The global nature of environmental challenges requires collective action on a worldwide scale. When individuals and organizations from different countries join forces to pursue sustainability, it fosters international cooperation. It helps address global issues such as climate change, biodiversity loss, and pollution.

LONG-TERM TRANSFORMATION

Collectively promoting sustainability represents a powerful mechanism for enacting lasting and positive change. It goes beyond short-term trends or isolated efforts, fostering enduring transformations that benefit the present and future generations.

Individuals actively participate in a global movement toward a more sustainable and environmentally conscious planet by supporting eco-friendly initiatives and businesses. This collective action harnesses personal choices and actions to effect constructive and enduring transformations, ultimately contributing to a world that thrives for the well-being of posterity.

SPREADING AWARENESS ABOUT SUSTAINABLE PRACTICES

The journey for creating a significant global impact doesn't stop with individual actions; it must expand and resonate on a much broader scale. While it begins with individuals adopting sustainable practices, the transformation requires reaching and inspiring many people.

Individuals can serve as trailblazers by embracing eco-friendly habits like reducing energy consumption, supporting sustainable products, or practicing waste reduction in their daily routines. However, for these changes to have the profound global impact they deserve, they must extend their reach and influence to the masses.

Awareness plays a pivotal role in this process. It serves as the catalyst that propels the expansion of sustainable practices. It acts as the spark that ignites a collective movement toward responsible living and environmental stewardship. When individuals become aware of our environmental challenges and the available solutions, they are more likely to join the cause, advocate for change, and inspire others to follow suit.

Awareness takes the seeds of change planted at the individual level and nurtures their growth into a flourishing forest of collective action. It transforms isolated efforts into a global movement for sustainability, where each person's contribution, no matter how modest, contributes to the momentum of the more significant cause. This exemplifies the transformative power of awareness in our quest for a more sustainable and environmentally conscious planet.

At its essence, creating awareness about sustainable practices involves illuminating people on the pressing environmental challenges confronting our world today. It means shedding light on climate change, deforestation, plastic pollution, and biodiversity loss. It's about conveying that these challenges are not remote problems but urgent crises affecting everyone.

Awareness campaigns serve as a channel, providing the knowledge and tools essential for empowering individuals to take action. They educate people about the ramifications of their daily decisions, be it the carbon footprint of their transportation choices, the influence of their dietary preferences on land use, or the imperative to reduce single-use plastic waste. This knowledge furnishes individuals with the comprehension of how their choices can either contribute to exacerbating these global issues or serve as mitigation measures.

Creating awareness for sustainable practices extends beyond knowledge; it cultivates a profound sense of personal responsibility and moral obligation. It prompts individuals to acknowledge that they play a role in safeguarding the environment and ensuring a habitable planet for future generations. This sense of duty is a potent motivator, compelling individuals to make sustainable choices and inspiring them to advocate for systemic change on a grander scale.

Spreading awareness about sustainable practices is a critical step toward making a global impact and nurturing a more environmentally conscious world. It encompasses a multifaceted approach, blending education, sharing, and active engagement across various platforms. Here's a comprehensive guide on how individuals and organizations can effectively disseminate awareness about sustainability, with real-world examples to illustrate each point:

Personal Commitment: Begin with personal dedication. For example, an individual might start composting kitchen scraps and proudly share the success of their lush, nutrient-rich garden due to their composting efforts.

Education: Learn about environmental sustainability and share knowledge through blogs or social media platforms. For instance, a science enthusiast could create engaging content explaining the science behind climate change and its impacts.

Sharing Best Practices: Share personal experiences with sustainable practices. A family might document their journey to zero-waste living on a YouTube channel, offering practical tips to followers.

Leveraging Social Media and Platforms: Use platforms like Instagram to showcase eco-friendly lifestyle choices. A fashion influencer could promote sustainable brands and share stylish, eco-conscious outfit ideas.

Embracing Sustainable Lifestyle Choices: Document daily eco-friendly habits. A commuter might post about their switch from driving to biking, highlighting the health and environmental benefits.

Informed Decision-Making: Share product reviews and recommendations based on sustainability. A tech enthusiast could compare the environmental impact of different gadgets, encouraging others to make eco-conscious tech choices.

Continuous Evaluation: Share updates on your sustainability journey, including challenges and solutions. A blogger might discuss their journey to reduce plastic use, emphasizing the learning process and adjustments made.

Collaboration: Organize or participate in local clean-up events and share the impact on social media. A community group might highlight how collective action can beautify neighborhoods and raise awareness about littering.

Advocacy: Support environmental NGOs and promote their campaigns. An environmental advocate could use their platform to raise funds and awareness for reforestation projects, demonstrating the importance of conservation efforts.

Leading by Example: Showcase the benefits of sustainable living through personal experiences. A chef might create a series of sustainable cooking videos emphasizing how delicious and accessible eco-friendly recipes can be.[35]

The dissemination of awareness about sustainable practices unfolds through a multi-pronged approach, with real-world examples illustrating each point. Through these collective endeavors, a global impact can be realized, propelling the transition toward a more sustainable and environmentally conscious planet.

HOLISTIC APPROACH TO SUSTAINABLE LIVING

> *"The ultimate test of man's conscience may be his willingness to sacrifice something today for future generations whose words of thanks will not be heard."*
>
> —Gaylord Nelson

EMBRACING A SUSTAINABLE LIFESTYLE IS A HOLISTIC APPROACH TO living that goes beyond isolated actions. It involves making interconnected choices and adopting eco-conscious habits that collectively contribute to a more environmentally responsible world. This comprehensive commitment encompasses waste reduction, energy conservation, eco-friendly transportation, sus-

35 https://pachamama.org/environmental-awareness

tainable dietary choices, ethical consumption, and responsible water management.

Each element is intertwined with the others, creating a synergistic impact that fosters a more balanced relationship between individuals and the planet. In this interconnected journey, individuals play a pivotal role in reducing their environmental footprint and nurturing a greener, healthier future for all.

Sustainable living emphasizes waste reduction, which involves recycling and composting while minimizing single-use plastics. These actions significantly reduce waste sent to landfills, alleviating the strain on ecosystems.

Concurrently, conserving energy is crucial. Simple steps like using energy-efficient appliances, weatherproofing homes, and practicing energy conservation led to a noticeable decrease in overall energy consumption. Supporting renewable energy sources further reinforces the commitment to reducing one's carbon footprint.

Transportation choices are intimately linked to sustainability. Opting for eco-friendly modes of transportation, such as public transit, carpooling, cycling, or walking, reduces greenhouse gas emissions and promotes healthier lifestyles. For those requiring personal vehicles, transitioning to electric or hybrid options aligns with sustainable transportation practices.

Food choices have far-reaching environmental consequences. A sustainable diet involves consuming locally sourced, organic, and seasonal foods whenever possible. Reducing meat consumption, especially beef, significantly lowers the carbon footprint of one's diet. Combating food waste and supporting sustainable farming practices are integral components of a sustainable approach to nourishment.

In the realm of consumer goods, sustainable living encompasses thoughtful and ethical purchasing decisions. Prioritizing durable, repairable, and environmentally friendly products is critical. Supporting businesses that uphold ethical sourcing and fair labor practices ensures that consumer choices align with sustainability principles.

Water conservation is another vital aspect of sustainable living. Simple measures like fixing leaks, adopting low-flow fixtures, and practicing efficient water use contribute to the responsible management of this finite resource.

Ultimately, a sustainable lifestyle is a dynamic and interconnected commitment. It involves continuously assessing and adjusting personal choices to align with sustainability goals and values. Rather than isolated actions, it's a holistic approach to daily living that promotes a more harmonious relationship between individuals and the planet.

Sustainable living recognizes the interconnectedness of various aspects of life, from waste reduction and energy conservation to transportation, food choices, consumer goods, and water management. It represents a comprehensive commitment to responsible living that benefits individuals and the environment, working together for a more sustainable and balanced world.[36]

CONCLUSION

THIS CHAPTER HAS GUIDED US THROUGH THE ESSENTIAL ELEMENTS of advancing environmental sustainability at the individual and collective levels. Our journey began with a focus on individuals' pivotal role in shaping a more sustainable future for our planet. We explored various interconnected choices that wield substantial influence, from waste reduction and resource conservation to

36 https://www.masterclass.com/articles/how-to-conserve-natural-resources

support for eco-friendly initiatives and businesses. Emphasis was placed on raising awareness about sustainable practices and inspiring others to join this cause. We discussed how understanding serves as the catalyst, propelling a collective movement toward responsible living and environmental stewardship. It transforms isolated efforts into a global sustainability movement.

We delved into the notion of adopting a sustainable lifestyle. This lifestyle encompasses waste reduction, energy conservation, eco-friendly transportation, sustainable dietary choices, ethical consumption, and responsible water management. This holistic approach acknowledges the interconnectedness of these life facets and advocates for a harmonious relationship between individuals and their environment. As we draw this chapter to a close, it becomes evident that sustainability is not a solitary pursuit but a shared commitment necessitating active involvement from individuals, businesses, and communities worldwide. We can collectively strive toward a more balanced and environmentally responsible world by persistently making conscientious choices and championing sustainable practices. The journey toward sustainability is ongoing, and our dedication to it invests in a brighter, greener future for generations to come.

CHAPTER ELEVEN

SOCIAL RESPONSIBILITY

Actions, not words, carry profound significance as they mark the beginning of our societal journey. Whether a huge corporation or a solitary individual, every step, favorable or detrimental, bears repercussions. This is where the concept of social responsibility emerges.

Social responsibility, a moral compass, urges all organizational and personal entities to pursue the greater good and refrain from harming society and the environment. While it frequently finds its discourse in the corporate realm, it transcends to encompass all segments of society. The fundamental premise it hinges upon is the realization that our actions reverberate through others and to be socially responsible. We must act in ways that enrich society while minimizing detriment.

For corporations, social responsibility entails a mission that surpasses profit maximization. It involves assessing the impact of their operations on the communities they serve, the environment, and the well-being of their workforce. By embracing social responsibility, corporations can become catalysts for positive societal change, establishing trust with their stakeholders and augmenting their reputation.

Individuals, too, hold a pivotal role in social responsibility. Each person's actions, from their treatment of others to their choices as consumers, collectively mold the prosperity of their communities and the planet. Adhering to social responsibility as an individual translates to acting with empathy, integrity, and a sense of obligation toward others. It can be as straightforward as volunteering for a local charitable organization, making environmentally conscious decisions, or endorsing equitable trade practices.

Social responsibility significantly influences our lives, impacting our choices and actions profoundly. It functions as a moral guide in our personal lives, directing us toward decisions that contribute to community and global betterment. It instills empathy and compassion, encouraging acts of kindness, support for charitable causes, and voluntary service. On a personal level, embracing social responsibility cultivates ethical conduct and integrity, strengthening interpersonal relationships and building trust within our social circles.

The concept extends to our environmental footprint in our personal lives. Making eco-conscious choices, such as waste reduction, energy conservation, and support for sustainability, plays a crucial role in preserving and improving the environment, ensuring a healthier planet for future generations. In our professional lives, social responsibility is equally significant. For businesses and organizations, it goes beyond profit-seeking, encompassing a commitment to the well-being of employees, stakeholders, and society. Social responsibility at work involves promoting fairness in employment practices, environmental care, and community philanthropy.

For individuals in professional roles, social responsibility means ethical decision-making and dedication to positive outcomes. It entails considering the welfare of all stakeholders, from customers and employees to shareholders and the public. Operating with social responsibility as a guiding principle helps professionals establish trust, enhance their reputation, and contribute to the sustainability of their industries and society.

Social responsibility is indispensable for infusing our lives with purpose and making a meaningful impact on the world. It reminds us that our actions have profound consequences, and by embracing them wholeheartedly, we not only improve our lives but also play a pivotal role in fostering a more just, compassionate, and sustainable world.[37]

GIVING BACK TO THE COMMUNITY

> *"Service to others is the rent you pay for your room here on Earth."*
>
> —Muhammad Ali

THE FUNDAMENTAL CONCEPT OF "GIVING BACK TO THE COMMUNITY" underscores the core tenets of social responsibility, encapsulating the idea of actively contributing to enhancing one's local community, whether the place of residence or operation.

37 https://www.humanrightscareers.com/issues/what-is-social-responsibility/

This concept emphasizes the interconnectedness of individuals and their communities, stressing responsibility and empathy toward those who share geographical or social proximity. It is a robust expression of social responsibility, signifying a dedication to forging a more equitable and supportive society.

Rooted in the principles of social responsibility, giving back to the community signifies a dedicated commitment to actively improve the welfare and advancement of the local community where one resides or operates. This commitment to giving back finds expression in various ways, with its core revolving around providing support, resources, and aid to address the unique challenges and needs encountered by the community.

At its essence, giving back to the community underscores a genuine aspiration to generate a positive influence beyond one's immediate sphere of influence. It epitomizes a sense of responsibility and empathy toward those with a common geographical or social context. This concept is grounded in the acknowledgment that no individual or entity exists in isolation; the community's well-being is intrinsically intertwined with the well-being of its members.

Giving back can take diverse forms, encompassing volunteering of time and skills, offering financial assistance to local charities and organizations, participating in projects aimed at community development, or sharing knowledge and expertise to address community issues. It can also involve backing educational endeavors, healthcare services, environmental conservation initiatives, and endeavors to mitigate social disparities.

Giving back to the community exemplifies a robust demonstration of social responsibility. It reflects a pledge to craft a more just, supportive, and dynamic society. This practice not only fortifies the connections within a community but also contributes to the overall betterment of the wider world. Through giving back, individuals and organizations fulfill a crucial role in initiating positive and enduring transformations while promoting a shared sense of duty toward the well-being of others and the communities they call home.

EMPOWERING SOCIAL RESPONSIBILITY WITH VOLUNTEERING

"Volunteers do not necessarily have the time; they just have the heart."

—Elizabeth Andrew

Volunteering is a foundational principle of social responsibility, embodying the fundamental idea that individuals contribute to the welfare of their communities and society. It entails dedicating one's time, skills, and energy to partake in various projects, initiatives actively, and causes that resonate with personal values and passions.

At its core, volunteering translates empathy into tangible action, signifying a commitment to create a positive impact. It underscores the belief that every individual wields unique talents and resources that can be harnessed for the betterment of others. By offering time and skills, volunteers contribute to the specific project at hand and the broader aspiration of nurturing a more compassionate and just society.

Volunteering transcends mere altruism; it operates as a dynamic exchange with numerous benefits. For volunteers, it offers a platform for personal growth and development. Volunteering often results in acquiring new skills, exposure to fresh perspectives, and a deepened comprehension of diverse social issues. It is potent for fostering confidence, enhancing self-esteem, and nurturing a sense of purpose.

From the perspective of the community and organizations, volunteering plays a transformative role. Nonprofits, community groups, and charitable organizations rely heavily on the support of volunteers to fulfill their missions. Volunteers augment these organizations' ability to serve their beneficiaries more efficiently. They provide the essential human capital required to execute crucial tasks, from delivering meals to older people to mentoring at-risk youth or engaging in environmental conservation endeavors.

Volunteering nurtures a sense of social cohesion and unity within communities. It unites people from various backgrounds under the common banner of a shared objective. This collective sense of purpose fosters stronger connections, heightened resilience, and a heightened awareness of shared responsibility for community well-being.

Volunteering is a cornerstone of social responsibility because it embodies the principle that individuals can enact positive change. It represents a proactive approach to addressing societal issues, affirming that collective efforts can exert a profound and enduring impact on the world regardless of scale. Through volunteering, individuals emerge as active agents of change, shaping a brighter and more compassionate future for both themselves and the communities they serve.

FINANCIAL FORM OF VOLUNTEERING

"No one has ever become poor by giving."

—Anne Frank

Donations, often regarded as a financial facet of volunteering, constitute a substantial and complementary dimension of social responsibility. While volunteering primarily entails allocating time and skills, financial contributions through donations empower individuals and organizations to exert a direct and consequential influence by offering monetary support to nonprofit organizations, charities, and community initiatives.

The concept of financial donations as a form of volunteering emanates from the core belief that individuals possess the capacity to contribute not only through their involvement but also via their financial resources. This approach broadens the scope of social responsibility, encompassing a more comprehensive array of contributions.

A notable advantage of financial donations is their adaptability. They allow individuals to support various causes, spanning education, healthcare, environmental preservation, and poverty alleviation. Donations can be allocated to the areas most urgently required, addressing pressing issues swiftly and effectively.

Donations are indispensable lifelines for numerous nonprofit organizations, equipping them with the means to sustain and expand their programs. These financial contributions facilitate the procurement of essential resources, the recruitment of skilled professionals, and the development of novel initiatives. Consequently, donations can significantly enhance the impact of volunteer endeavors. For instance, a volunteer-driven tutoring program for underprivileged children can experience substantial benefits from financial donations. These funds can be used to acquire educational materials, extend the program's reach, and enhance its effectiveness.

Donations also fulfill a critical function in fortifying the nonprofit sector. Organizations can plan for the long term by delivering a stable funding source and constructing a more robust infrastructure. This, in turn, assures that nonprofits can continue to serve their communities with effectiveness and tackle pressing societal challenges.

Financial donations, functioning as a manifestation of volunteering, emerge as a potent and versatile channel for advancing social responsibility. They enhance and supplement hands-on volunteering by providing resources that substantially amplify the influence of volunteer endeavors. Be it one-time contributions, regular donations, or strategic partnerships, donating signals a firm dedication to cultivating enduring and positive change in the world. When fused with the potential of volunteerism, financial donations are integral to a holistic approach to social responsibility. This empowers individuals and organizations to deliver a considerable and lasting impact on their communities.

ROLE OF PARTNERSHIPS IN VOLUNTEERING

Forming partnerships is a dynamic and vital component of volunteering and social responsibility. Partnerships go beyond individual efforts and organizations working in isolation, creating synergistic relationships that amplify the impact of volunteer initiatives and community service.

Partnerships in the context of volunteering involve collaborative arrangements between various stakeholders, such as individuals, businesses, nonprofit organizations, and governmental agencies. These alliances are often based on shared values and a joint commitment to addressing societal issues, ranging from environmental conservation to education, healthcare, and poverty alleviation.

There are several critical aspects of forming partnerships as a part of volunteering:

Leveraging Expertise: Partnerships allow organizations and individuals to tap into each other's expertise and resources. Businesses may provide pro bono services, such as legal or marketing support, to nonprofit organizations, enhancing their operational efficiency and impact. Likewise, nonprofits can offer valuable insights into community needs and issues that businesses can address.

Resource Sharing: Partnerships often involve sharing resources, both tangible and intangible. This can include sharing office space, equipment, or technology. Such sharing reduces overhead costs for nonprofits, allowing them to allocate more resources directly to their mission.

Amplifying Reach: Collaborative efforts through partnerships can lead to broader outreach and increased community impact. Multiple organizations can reach a more extensive and diverse audience when they come together. This collective reach can lead to larger beneficiaries and a more comprehensive approach to tackling social issues.

Collective Problem Solving: Partnerships promote collective problem-solving. Different perspectives and skills come together to address complex issues. This diversity of thought often leads to more innovative and effective solutions.

Sustainability: Partnerships contribute to the long-term sustainability of volunteer initiatives. The pooling of resources and expertise creates a more resilient infrastructure, ensuring that projects can continue despite challenges.

Community Engagement: Forming partnerships also fosters community engagement. Collaborating with others demonstrates a shared commitment to community welfare, encouraging community members to become actively involved in addressing local issues.

For example, a local business and a food bank partnership may involve the business providing financial donations and volunteers to help with food distribution. This collaboration ensures a steady supply of resources and engages the local workforce in community service.

Forming partnerships as part of volunteering is a strategic approach that enhances the effectiveness and sustainability of volunteer efforts. It brings together various stakeholders, allowing them to leverage their combined resources and expertise to address complex social issues. These alliances are a testament to the collective power of social responsibility, reflecting a commitment to creating positive change and fostering a more compassionate and equitable society.

MAKING A DIFFERENCE THROUGH SKILL-BASED VOLUNTEERING

Skill-based volunteering, a highly specialized form of community service, harnesses an individual's talents, expertise, and professional skills to benefit nonprofit organizations, charities, and community initiatives. Diverging from traditional volunteering that may involve tasks not demanding specialized skills, skill-based volunteering revolves around the principle that everyone has something of value to contribute.

This approach encourages individuals to pinpoint their specific skills, such as marketing, design, legal proficiency, IT, finance, or other professional domains. Once these skills are identified, volunteers can actively seek opportunities where their expertise can effect meaningful change.

A primary advantage of skill-based volunteering is the capacity to directly and significantly impact the organizations and causes they support. Through rendering expert-level aid, volunteers assist these entities in operating more efficiently, broadening their reach, or more effectively addressing complex challenges. For instance, a graphic designer can enhance a nonprofit's marketing materials, a lawyer can provide legal counsel, or a web developer can revamp an organization's website to improve user experience and outreach.

Skill-based volunteering creates a mutually beneficial relationship. Nonprofits gain access to specialized skills they might not otherwise afford, while volunteers undergo personal and professional development. These experiences often lead to acquiring new skills, expanding one's network, and understanding various social issues. It's a symbiotic interaction that fosters a sense of satisfaction and achievement for the individual volunteer and the organization they assist.

Skill-based volunteering is highly adaptable, offering opportunities for short-term and long-term commitments, remote or in-person engagement, and varying levels of involvement. This adaptability permits individuals to align their volunteer endeavors with their schedules and interests.

In an ever-evolving world, skill-based volunteering is a dynamic and impactful means for individuals to contribute to their communities and society. It underscores that the most potent contributions arise from financial donations or manual labor and each individual's knowledge, expertise, and professional insight. It exemplifies the belief that skills are not solely assets for personal success but potent instruments for catalyzing positive change in the world.[38]

38 https://benevity.com/resources/skills-based-volunteering/

FOSTERING COMMUNITY ENGAGEMENT AND COLLABORATION

> *"Community engagement is about people dealing with the conditions that we live in on a daily basis. We must engage with those issues to make our communities better."*
>
> —Tanya R. Cochran

Social responsibility is not a solitary path but a collective journey, a harmonious orchestration of individual endeavors that resounds throughout communities and society. It signifies the unwavering dedication of both individuals and organizations to confront the pressing social challenges that characterize our era. However, the genuine potency of social responsibility does not solely reside in individual actions but flourishes within the vibrancy of community involvement, cooperation, and shared triumphs.

Promoting community engagement and collaboration is a fundamental tenet of effective volunteerism and social responsibility. It nurtures a sense of unity and shared responsibility within a community to confront pressing societal issues. This approach encompasses key elements: facilitating discussions, partnering with fellow community members, and acknowledging and celebrating community accomplishments.

FACILITATING CONVERSATIONS

Significant change often commences with open and candid dialogues. Encouraging discussions within a community assists in identifying shared concerns, common objectives, and possible solutions to critical societal challenges. These conversations furnish a platform for community members to voice their worries, share their experiences, and present diverse viewpoints. By endorsing active and respectful communication, volunteers can construct a sense of cohesion and comprehension among community members, paving the route to effective issue resolution.

COLLABORATING WITH COMMUNITY MEMBERS

Collaborative endeavors hold the potential to drive substantial societal change. Encouraging individuals, organizations, and businesses to collaborate fosters a unified method of addressing challenges. Volunteers can act as pivotal mediators, bridging divides among various entities. Cooperative projects harness community members' combined strengths and resources, allowing for more comprehensive and enduring solutions to societal issues.

RECOGNIZING ACHIEVEMENTS

Commemorating community achievements stands as a pivotal facet of community engagement. Acknowledging and spotlighting the constructive impacts of volunteer initiatives, community undertakings, and individual contributions can motivate others to become involved. It also nurtures a sense of pride and solidarity within the community. Recognizing the achievements of a local environmental conservation initiative or celebrating the triumphs of community members who have surmounted adversity, these acknowledgments fortify community spirit and stimulate continued engagement.

CELEBRATING DIVERSITY

Communities are the epitome of diversity, and celebrating this diversity is essential to community engagement. Promoting inclusivity and honoring the distinctive contributions of various community groups fosters a sense of belonging and unity. Volunteers can cultivate a more inclusive and harmonious environment where every voice is cherished by observing the community's cultural, social, and demographic richness.

YOUTH AND FUTURE GENERATIONS

Encouraging community engagement also entails engaging and empowering the youth and future generations. Encouraging young individuals to engage in community service and social responsibility imparts a sense of civic duty and equips them to tackle future societal issues.

In practical terms, community engagement and collaboration might encompass hosting town hall meetings, establishing community task forces, orchestrating volunteer-led projects, and developing initiatives that mirror the collective aspirations of the community.

Promoting community engagement and collaboration primarily involves cultivating a robust, interconnected community that collaborates to confront the most pressing societal challenges. Volunteers can play a pivotal role in shaping a more empathetic, united, and action-oriented society that actively addresses the obstacles they encounter through fostering open dialogues, encouraging cooperation, acknowledging accomplishments, and exalting diversity.

SUPPORTING WORTHY CAUSES FOR A STRONGER SOCIETY

Supporting worthy causes is a fundamental embodiment of social responsibility, signifying a dedication to positive change in vital matters. It goes beyond the confines of financial donations or volunteerism; it epitomizes a proactive strategy of comprehending, advocating for, and engaging with significant causes for individuals and communities. This support comprises several vital facets: delving into community needs, participating in and propagating events, and kindling the inspiration that encourages others to partake in community service.

RESEARCHING COMMUNITY NEEDS

A key integral step in endorsing worthy causes is the meticulous exploration to identify and grasp the most pressing concerns within a community. This exploration entails evaluating the necessities, difficulties, and prospects that exist. It frequently encompasses accumulating data, executing surveys, and interfacing with local stakeholders to obtain insights into what genuinely matters to the community. Through this exploration, individuals and organizations can guarantee that their endeavors are well-informed and channeled toward the most pivotal domains.

PARTICIPATING IN AND PROMOTING EVENTS

Engaging with worthy causes commonly entails active involvement in community events, campaigns, and ventures that straightforwardly address these causes. This involved engagement exhibits commitment and unity with the cause, whether it encompasses volunteering at a local food drive, participating in a charity marathon, or organizing a fundraising event. In addition, promoting such events through social media, word-of-mouth, and alternative channels enhances their impact by heightening awareness and encouraging more individuals to become involved.

INSPIRING AND MOTIVATING OTHERS

One of the most influential facets of backing worthy causes is the ability to kindle inspiration and spur others to participate in community service. Through personal accounts of impact, vigorous advocacy, or leadership by example, individuals can develop the spirit of volunteerism and social responsibility in others. By disseminating their experiences and allegiance to a cause, they set a ripple effect that inspires more individuals to act and contribute to improving their communities.

In practical terms, advocating for worthy causes might encompass initiatives such as organizing community cleanup endeavors, participating in fundraisers for local charities, or supporting educational programs in underserved regions. The quintessence lies in harmonizing individual values and interests with the community's requirements and actively participating in endeavors that craft a substantial difference.

Supporting worthy causes is a pivotal element of social responsibility that exemplifies the essence of community involvement and proactive issue resolution. By researching needs, actively participating in and advocating for events, and rousing others to participate, individuals and organizations can construct a unified front against pressing social challenges, fostering a more robust and compassionate society.

ETHICAL DECISION MAKING

Ethical decision-making is a pivotal element of social responsibility, transcending the boundaries of business and personal life. It entails comprehending ethical principles and frameworks and actively incorporating these ethics into our decision-making processes. Furthermore, it is an iterative journey requiring constant introspection and enhancing our choices. Let's explore this concept comprehensively, delving into instances of its application in both personal and professional contexts.

GRASPING ETHICAL PRINCIPLES AND FRAMEWORKS

A comprehensive understanding of ethical principles and frameworks forms the bedrock of ethical decision-making, serving as a moral compass to navigate the choices we encounter in our personal and professional lives. These principles, which encompass attributes like integrity, empathy, fairness, and honesty, provide the foundational values that guide our ethical considerations.

SIGNIFICANCE OF ETHICAL PRINCIPLES

Ethical principles act as a moral compass, guiding our personal and professional decision-making. They define right from wrong, providing clarity during moral dilemmas. Integrity, for example, underscores the value of honesty and ethical behavior. Abiding by integrity implies a commitment to truthfulness and transparency.

ETHICAL REASONING FRAMEWORKS

Ethical frameworks provide structured approaches to resolve moral dilemmas and make ethical choices. They encompass various philosophies like utilitarianism, deontology, virtue ethics, and care ethics. These systems offer systematic methods to analyze and address ethical challenges. In the corporate realm, a company may adopt a deontological approach, adhering to specific rules and principles in its code of conduct to ensure ethical decisions in compliance with fairness and the law.

BUSINESS ETHICS

Within the business world, ethical principles and frameworks play a pivotal role in ethical decision-making. Business ethics employs these principles to guide actions, decisions, and behavior. Employees and leaders alike rely on these principles to navigate difficult situations. Consider a company contemplating advertising a product. A profound grasp of ethical principles such as honesty and fairness will steer the company toward responsible and ethical advertising practices.

BALANCING ETHICAL PRINCIPLES

Ethical decision-making often involves the task of balancing multiple principles. Take healthcare, for instance, where respecting patient confidentiality is a core ethical principle. Yet, at times, this can conflict with the principle of beneficence, which obliges healthcare professionals to act in the best interests of their patients. In these instances, healthcare providers must thoughtfully weigh the implications of both principles to make decisions that honor patient rights and promote their well-being.

ETHICAL PRINCIPLES IN PERSONAL LIFE

The influence of ethical principles extends beyond professional boundaries into personal life. Honesty, for example, is a guiding principle in everyday scenarios, urging individuals to be truthful in interactions with family and friends. The focus of empathy encourages considering the feelings and perspectives of others in personal decision-making. In relationships, fairness ensures equitable treatment for all parties involved.

A profound understanding of ethical principles and frameworks forms the cornerstone of ethical decision-making, steering our choices in both personal and professional spheres. These principles offer clarity, set standards of conduct, and enable individuals and organizations to navigate the complexities of ethical dilemmas, ultimately contributing to a more responsible and compassionate society.

INFUSING ETHICAL DELIBERATIONS

Infusing ethical considerations into decision-making is an integral part of practicing social responsibility, and it requires a conscious effort to apply ethical principles throughout the decision-making process. This process is not limited to business; it extends into our personal lives, influencing our choices to ensure they align with our ethical values.

EMBRACING ETHICAL PRINCIPLES

The process of infusing ethical considerations initiates with the wholehearted adoption of ethical principles such as integrity, fairness, and honesty into the decision-making process. For instance, within a corporate context, a decision-maker may precede fair labor practices throughout the supply chain, even if it entails slightly higher costs. This reflects an unwavering commitment to ethical values, including fairness, justice, and social responsibility.

BALANCING ETHICAL DILEMMAS

Ethical deliberations frequently entail the art of harmonizing competing values. Imagine a company grappling with whether to prioritize profit maximization or environmental sustainability. Ethical decision-makers meticulously evaluate their core principles to strike a harmonious equilibrium.

TRANSPARENCY AND ACCOUNTABILITY

The incorporation of ethical considerations necessitates transparency and accountability in the decision-making process. Open and forthright communication ensures that all stakeholders comprehend a decision's moral reasoning. In business, transparent reporting and the acknowledgment of decision accountability are emblematic of ethical leadership.

Integrating ethical considerations into decision-making is a purposeful and forward-looking endeavor to align one's actions with ethical and moral values. It necessitates a comprehensive grasp of ethical principles and the courage to champion them, even when confronted with competing interests or adversities. By threading ethical principles throughout decision-making, individuals and organizations advocate social responsibility and contribute to a more honest and conscientious society.[39]

CONTINUAL ASSESSMENT OF ETHICAL DECISION-MAKING

Continual assessment of ethical decision-making is vital to social responsibility, underscoring that ethical considerations are dynamic but ever-evolving. It's a journey of self-awareness, improvement, and adaptation in the corporate world and our personal lives. Here, we delve into the key elements of this practice and its significance.

REFLECTION AND SELF-EXAMINATION

Continual assessment necessitates regular self-reflection and examination of the ethical principles and values that guide our decision-making. This introspection allows us to understand how our principles may evolve and adapt to changing circumstances.

39 https://www.toolshero.com/tag/ethical-decision-making/

ADAPTING TO EVOLVING CIRCUMSTANCES

As circumstances and societal norms change, ethical considerations must also adapt. In the corporate context, a company may need to review and adjust its ethical policies and practices to align with evolving sustainability objectives or changing consumer expectations, such as adopting greener practices in response to heightened environmental awareness.

ACCOUNTABILITY AND RESPONSIVENESS

Continual assessment reinforces accountability. It encourages individuals and organizations to acknowledge and take responsibility for any ethical missteps or shortcomings in the past and to adjust their course of action to avoid repeating such mistakes.

Continually assessing ethical decision-making is an ongoing and adaptive process that aligns our ethical compass with evolving values and circumstances. It promotes accountability, responsiveness, and ethical growth in the corporate world and within ourselves. This practice is at the heart of social responsibility, ensuring that our actions and choices reflect our commitment to a more ethical, responsible, and compassionate society.

Ethical decision-making is a multifaceted and evolving facet of social responsibility that leaves its mark on our personal and professional lives. We contribute to a more honest and responsible society while preserving our integrity and moral values through comprehension of ethical principles, seamless integration into decisions, and perpetual introspection of our ethical choices.

INCORPORATING ETHICAL BUSINESS PRACTICES

"Businesses have a social responsibility and should be committed to ethical practices, not just profit."

—Sir Richard Branson

Adopting ethical business practices is a pivotal step in the social responsibility journey. It involves the deliberate integration of ethical considerations within an organization's operations, ensuring that ethical principles are not just ideals but integral parts of the company's identity. This process includes implementing policies, providing supply chain transparency, and continually evaluating and improving business practices. By adopting ethical business practices, organizations cultivate a strong moral compass that guides decision-making and aligns actions with personal and societal values.

Here are some crucial steps for adopting ethical business practices:

INCORPORATING ETHICAL POLICIES

Initiating ethical business practices commences with the formulation and implementation of ethical policies. These policies delineate the ethical values and principles that the organization wholeheartedly embraces. For instance, a company might devise a code of conduct emphasizing honesty, transparency, and respect in every facet of its business dealings.

ENSURING TRANSPARENT SUPPLY CHAINS

A fundamental belief of ethical business practices is supply chain transparency. This entails tracing the origins and production processes of an organization's products or materials. By ensuring transparency, businesses can detect and rectify unethical practices, such as child labor or environmental exploitation. Such transparency also empowers consumers to make informed choices.

CONTINUOUS ASSESSMENT AND ENHANCEMENT

Ethical business practices are far from static; they necessitate ongoing evaluation and enhancement. Organizations must periodically scrutinize their operations to pinpoint areas where ethical considerations can be more effectively integrated. For instance, a company may continually evaluate its environmental impact, persistently striving to diminish its carbon footprint through sustainable practices.

FOSTERING A ROBUST MORAL COMPASS

Adopting ethical business practices transcends mere compliance, aiming to cultivate a robust moral compass within the organization. This moral compass guides decision-making across all levels, ensuring that choices consistently resonate with individual values and ethical principles. It profoundly influences actions, strategies, and interactions with employees, customers, and the broader community.

Consider a clothing manufacturer ardently committed to ethical business practices. The company ardently implements policies that give paramount importance to fair labor practices, guaranteeing equitable compensation and safe working conditions for its employees. The attainment of supply chain transparency is rigorously pursued by tracing the origins of raw materials, such as cotton, and ascertaining their sources adhere to sustainability and responsible management. The company relentlessly pursues sustainable and eco-friendly manufacturing processes through recurrent evaluations. This company's adoption of ethical practices fosters a robust moral compass within its organization and forges a profound connection with consumers who esteem ethical and sustainable fashion.

Adopting ethical business practices is an integral component of social responsibility, symbolic of an organization's unswerving commitment to instill ethical and moral values at the heart of its operations. By instituting ethical policies, ensuring supply chain transparency, and perpetually evaluating and enhancing business practices, organizations steer by a moral compass that guides them in making decisions that faithfully mirror their values and the broader ethics of society. This approach engenders benefits not solely for the organization but also for the communities it serves and the world.

PILLAR OF SOCIAL RESPONSIBILITY

> *"Advocacy can drive change, change can drive progress, and progress can drive a brighter future for all."*
>
> —Ellen J. Kullman

Advocating for change and using influence for good is the third integral aspect of social responsibility. It transcends personal and organizational boundaries, taking a proactive stance in addressing social and environmental issues. This approach involves identifying pertinent issues, developing strategies and initiatives to raise awareness, and collaborating with various stakeholders, from individuals and organizations to government entities.

The critical components of advocating for change include:

Issue Identification

Advocating for change starts with identifying significant social and environmental issues that demand attention. This requires staying attuned to emerging challenges and recognizing areas where positive change can be achieved. For instance, it is identifying a need to address food insecurity in a local community.

Awareness-Raising Strategies

Once an issue is identified, advocating for change entails creating strategies and initiatives to raise awareness. These strategies can encompass various actions, such as organizing awareness campaigns, conducting educational workshops, utilizing social media to amplify messages, and collaborating with media outlets to shed light on the issue.

Collaboration with Stakeholders

Effective advocacy relies on collaboration. This involves forming partnerships with diverse stakeholders, including other organizations, individuals, and government entities. Collaborative efforts pool resources, knowledge, and influence, enabling a more substantial impact. For example, a nonprofit organization addressing homelessness may collaborate with local government agencies to create comprehensive solutions.

Let's take a look at a corporate and individual example of this:

CORPORATE ADVOCACY

A socially responsible corporation may identify a pressing environmental issue, such as plastic pollution, and launch a public campaign to raise awareness. They collaborate with environmental organizations, partner with government agencies to promote recycling initiatives and adopt eco-friendly packaging practices to mitigate the problem.

INDIVIDUAL ADVOCACY

An individual committed to social responsibility may identify a need for improved access to education in underserved communities. They can start by volunteering as a mentor, raising funds for educational resources, and collaborating with local schools and organizations to develop long-term educational programs.

Advocating for change and leveraging influence for good are dynamic and essential to social responsibility. Individuals and organizations can bring about meaningful change by identifying pertinent issues, devising awareness-raising strategies, and collaborating with stakeholders. This proactive approach to addressing societal challenges aligns with the principles of social responsibility and contributes to improving communities, society, and the world.

Power of Advocacy

Advocating for social causes extends beyond acknowledging issues; it actively involves creating awareness, sharing narratives, and leveraging personal and professional networks for the greater good. This multifaceted approach plays a crucial role in propelling positive change.

EDUCATION AS A CATALYST FOR CHANGE

As a potent catalyst for change, education empowers advocates. They take the initiative to educate themselves and others about the intricacies of social issues, delving into root causes, consequences, and potential solutions. Informed advocates become ambassadors for change, presenting compelling arguments and mobilizing support.

SHARING STORIES VIA SOCIAL MEDIA

Social media's transformative role in advocacy is undeniable. Advocates harness these platforms to share stories, experiences, and information. They raise awareness, engage in conversations, and foster community around their chosen causes. By utilizing the power of social media, advocates reach diverse and widespread audiences, amplifying their voices on a global scale. This impact is particularly profound in social justice, environmental concerns, and human rights movements.

LEVERAGING PERSONAL AND PROFESSIONAL NETWORKS

An advocate's network is one of their most influential tools. Advocates tap into their personal and professional connections to amplify the voices of marginalized communities. They leverage their influence to secure resources, engage decision-makers, and encourage others to join their cause. Whether through partnerships, collaborations, or merely by spreading the message within their circles, advocates generate a groundswell of support.

DRIVING POSITIVE CHANGE THROUGH INFLUENCE

Influence is the dynamic force behind advocating for social causes. It empowers advocates to effect tangible change by mobilizing resources, support, and action. Whether advocating for local change as an individual or pushing for systemic shifts as a global organization, influence propels the cause forward. It persuades policymakers, garners media attention, and inspires collective action, leading to substantial results.

Here are a few examples of effective advocacy:

Social Justice: Advocates for social justice use educational campaigns, social media, and their networks to spotlight systemic inequalities. Their goal is to transform discriminatory policies and promote inclusivity and equity.

Climate Change: Environmental advocates educate the public about the urgent need to address climate change. They use social media to amplify climate-related stories and build networks of organizations, scientists, and policymakers to drive eco-friendly policies.

Public Health: In public health advocacy, individuals and organizations educate communities about health issues, use social media to disseminate health information, and collaborate with healthcare professionals and governmental bodies to enhance healthcare access and policies.

Advocating for social causes is an active and multifaceted pursuit that employs education, storytelling, networks, and influence to drive positive change. It epitomizes the power of collective action and the unwavering commitment of individuals and organizations to create a more equitable, just, and compassionate world.[40]

FOSTERING EQUITY AND INCLUSION

> *"It is not our differences that divide us. It is our inability to recognize, accept, and celebrate those differences."*
>
> —Audre Lorde

PROMOTING DIVERSITY, EQUITY, AND INCLUSION IS A PROFOUND dedication to forging a fairer and more equitable society. This endeavor employs a multi-layered approach encompassing education, self-awareness, advocacy, policy implementation, and

40 https://onlinesocialwork.vcu.edu/blog/advocacy-in-social-work/

creating inclusive environments. This comprehensive strategy aims to challenge systemic discrimination and biases while nurturing a culture of empathy, understanding, and respect in both personal and professional domains.

CONFRONTING SYSTEMIC DISCRIMINATION AND BIAS

Initiating the journey toward diversity and inclusion commences with acknowledging systemic discrimination and biases affecting various communities. It embarks on an ongoing journey of learning and self-reflection. Individuals actively confront their personal preferences and assumptions, working diligently to unlearn prejudiced beliefs and grasp the experiences of marginalized groups. This process cultivates empathy and positions advocates as allies in the battle against discrimination.

ERADICATING SYSTEMIC BARRIERS

Advocates relentlessly dismantle systemic barriers and biases that obstruct equal access to opportunities and resources. They identify enduring systemic obstacles and ardently advocate for change. This advocacy entails collaboration with institutions, governments, and organizations to push for policy reforms that address inequalities.

ENFORCING INCLUSIVE POLICIES AND PRACTICES

Moving beyond advocacy, proactive measures are instituted to enforce inclusive policies and practices. This entails establishing frameworks and guidelines championing diversity and equity within organizations, institutions, and communities. This may involve adopting diversity-focused hiring policies, equitable wage practices, and mentorship programs in a corporate context. On a personal level, it could encompass backing local initiatives that champion inclusivity.

INSPIRING OTHERS TO PARTICIPATE

Advocates are pivotal in galvanizing others to partake in diversity and inclusion initiatives. Through disseminating knowledge, personal experiences, and resources, they ignite the passion of individuals and organizations to pursue a more equitable and inclusive society actively.

CULTIVATING AN INCLUSIVE ENVIRONMENT

One of the chief objectives in promoting diversity and inclusion is creating an inclusive environment that welcomes and appreciates individuals from all backgrounds. This environment celebrates diversity, fostering an atmosphere where diverse perspectives and experiences are shared freely. It is a space where individuals can express their identities and contribute to the community's progress.

NURTURING A CULTURE OF EMPATHY AND RESPECT

At the heart of diversity and inclusion efforts lies nurturing a culture marked by empathy, understanding, and respect. This culture permeates personal and professional spheres, underscoring the significance of treating individuals with dignity and recognizing their intrinsic worth. It is a culture that empowers individuals to confront discrimination and uphold the principles of equity and inclusion.

Here are some examples of diversity and inclusion advocacy:

WORKPLACE INCLUSIVITY

In a workplace unwavering in its commitment to diversity and inclusion, multifaceted programs are meticulously crafted to actively recruit, retain, and promote employees from underrepresented backgrounds. These inclusive initiatives encompass diverse aspects, including:

Strategic Recruitment Initiatives: The company ***proactively engages*** with diverse talent pools by participating in job fairs ***and*** specialized recruitment events and forming strategic alliances with organizations dedicated to connecting underrepresented groups with promising employment opportunities.

Diversity Training: Employees partake in comprehensive diversity and inclusion training programs that heighten their awareness regarding the importance of equity and inclusion. This training touches on themes such as unconscious bias, cultural proficiency, and the immense value of diverse perspectives.

Affinity Groups and Employee Resource Networks: The company creates affinity groups or employee resource networks that furnish a supportive community for individuals from underrepresented backgrounds. These groups may center around particular communities, such as LGBTQ+ employees, women, or racial and ethnic minorities, fostering a sense of belonging and shared purpose.

Mentorship and Sponsorship Initiatives: ***Mentorship and sponsorship programs are meticulously formulated to facilitate professional advancement***. These programs pair employees from underrepresented groups with more seasoned colleagues who provide invaluable guidance to advance their careers.

Fair Wage and Pay Equity Practices: The company institutes a robust commitment to fair compensation practices, guaranteeing that all employees receive equitable compensation, irrespective of their background. Regular pay equity audits are conducted to spot and rectify any wage discrepancies.[41]

EDUCATIONAL EQUITY

Advocates dedicated to educational equity tirelessly try ***to eradicate systemic barriers hindering quality education access***. Their comprehensive initiatives encompass various facets, such as:

Equitable Resource Allocation: Advocates champion equitable resource allocation within educational institutions, ensuring students in underserved communities have access to top-notch educators, up-to-date educational materials, and a secure learning environment.

Mentoring and Tutoring Programs: Initiatives are launched to ***give students in underserved communities*** access to mentors and tutors who provide indispensable academic support and guidance, nurturing their educational journeys.

College and Career Readiness Programs: Tailored programs are developed to prepare students for the rigors of college or career opportunities. This includes ***assisting*** in standardized testing, navigating college applications, and accessing financial aid resources.

Parent and Community Engagement: Advocates enthusiastically encourage the active participation of parents and communities in educational matters. This encompasses organizing

---

41 https://teambuilding.com/blog/inclusive-workplaces

workshops, meetings, and events that bolster collaboration between ***academic*** institutions and the families they serve.

COMMUNITY INITIATIVES

Advocates at the community level forge collaborations with local governments to instate policies and programs that cultivate inclusivity. These endeavors span a spectrum of initiatives, including:

Accessible Public Spaces: Advocates work with local authorities to guarantee that public spaces like parks, libraries, and transportation hubs are accessible to ***disabled individuals***. This may involve the installation of ramps, elevators, and provisions for those with mobility challenges.

Multilingual Services: To cater to the ***community's diversity***, advocates tirelessly strive to establish multilingual services in government offices, healthcare facilities, and public services. This encompasses the provision of interpreters, translated documents, and language assistance to cater to non-English speakers and break down language barriers.

Cultural Celebrations and Events: Promoting inclusivity entails organizing cultural celebrations, events, and festivals that acknowledge and celebrate the diverse ecosystem of the community. These gatherings provide platforms for individuals from various backgrounds to come together and share their cultural heritage.

Community Outreach: Advocates engage in far-reaching outreach efforts to connect with marginalized communities, ensuring their voices are heard and their needs are addressed by local government. This might entail conducting surveys, hosting town hall meetings, and advocating for community-driven solutions.

Promoting diversity, equity, and inclusion is a multifaceted endeavor that necessitates self-awareness, advocacy, and action. It aims to dismantle systemic discrimination, create inclusive environments, and cultivate a culture defined by empathy and respect. This unwavering commitment to equality and justice is integral to social responsibility, fostering a more harmonious and equitable world for all.

CONCLUSION

This chapter delves into social responsibility and ethical living, providing a comprehensive roadmap to nurture a fairer, more compassionate global community. It begins with the fundamental tenets of giving back to the community and supporting noble causes, underscoring the significance of research, community engagement, and volunteering as impactful tools. These actions have a ripple effect extending to helping organizations, contributing time, effort, and financial resources. They culminate in forging partnerships and cultivating an unwavering moral compass that aligns with personal values.

The journey doesn't stop there; it proceeds to delve into ethical decision-making, transcending the boundaries of personal and business domains. This practice hinges on a profound understanding of ethical principles, their application to daily choices, and a comprehensive evaluation of the societal, environmental, and economic consequences of decisions. It places a paramount emphasis on long-term sustainability and the judicious prioritization of ethical values.

The chapters continue with the vital advocacy for change and the strategic utilization of influence for the greater good. Advocates are proactive in identifying and championing pressing social and environmental issues. Their efforts involve raising awareness, sharing compelling narratives, and harnessing their personal and professional networks to amplify the voices of marginalized communities. This stands as a testament to the incredible potential of collective action and the profound influence individuals and organizations can wield on a global scale.

Lastly, the chapter underscores the profound importance of championing diversity, equity, and inclusion. The journey commences with an individual's self-awareness, encompassing a relentless commitment to challenging personal biases and actively striving to dismantle systemic barriers. Advocates ardently work toward creating inclusive environments that celebrate the vibrancy of diversity. This fosters a culture steeped in empathy, mutual understanding, and unwavering respect within personal and professional spheres.

The principles and insights expounded in this chapter act as a unifying compass, equally relevant for individuals and institutions. They lay the groundwork for social responsibility and ethical living, embodying the core tenets that underlie a society defined by fairness, empathy, and unity. This serves as a testament to the potential of each person to create tangible transformations. By embracing these principles wholeheartedly, we contribute collectively to a world where every action catalyzes positive change, making social responsibility an intrinsic part of our existence, transcending the realm of abstract theory.

CHAPTER TWELVE

CONCLUSION

In the preceding chapters, we've thoroughly explored the concept of 1% improvement and its transformative power. We've discovered how accumulating small, consistent efforts can lead to remarkable progress. As we conclude our journey, we will emphasize the broader implications of this philosophy.

The idea of the 1% improvement may appear deceptively simple, but it embodies the essence of personal development and enduring success. It's a reminder that significant change often begins with modest steps. It's the recognition that monumental goals can be attained through the daily pursuit of minor improvements.

"The journey of a thousand miles begins with one step."
—Lao Tzu

At its core, the notion of slight improvement involves the process of stimulating gradual, incremental modifications across various aspects of our lives. These changes may appear inconsequential, but their cumulative impact can be transformative when aggregated over time. The allure of minor improvements lies in their practicality and sustainability. They represent manageable, actionable steps accessible to anyone, serving as a feasible route to advancement.

Minor improvements starkly contrast the grand, sweeping gestures often associated with transformative change. While significant milestones are important, emphasizing minor improvements recognizes that monumental objectives can be reached through small, consistent, and sustainable adjustments. It involves breaking down complex aspirations into digestible, manageable fragments, essentially creating a roadmap that anyone can navigate.

The tenet of 1% improvement elevates the concept of minor improvements to another level. It revolves around the commitment to daily progress, striving for a 1% enhancement in various facets of life. While this 1% may seem marginal, it's a logical and attainable target that can be diligently pursued. The strength of this philosophy lies in its acknowledgment that persistent, incremental change proves more sustainable and effective than sporadic, drastic endeavors.

The notion of 1% improvement is founded on the belief that enduring change emerges from accumulating small daily efforts. It's a mindset that emphasizes progress over perfection. By pursuing a 1% increase each day, individuals are more likely to sustain their motivation, overcome setbacks, and, ultimately, reach their goals.

1% improvement transcends the bounds of self-development; it extends its application to virtually every facet of life, whether professional advancement, personal relationships, or broader global impact and sustainability. It is a universal principle, showcasing the transformative potential of consistency, perseverance, and the influence of minor, persistent strides.

In the preceding chapters leading up to this final section, we've observed how the philosophy of 1% improvement can be integrated into numerous aspects of life, guiding us on an odyssey of perpetual growth and self-betterment. It's not just a good theory; it deeply resonates with our inherent human nature. By embracing small, continuous change, we unlock the potential for enduring progress, reinforcing that each day presents an opportunity to draw closer to our finest selves.

JOURNEY OF CONTINUOUS GROWTH

In a world frequently consumed by the allure of instant gratification, the notion of 1% improvement serves as a poignant reminder of the beauty inherent in sustained effort and unwavering consistency. It's a testament to recognizing the potency of steadily accruing incremental progress. Our current age often fosters expectations of swift remedies and immediate outcomes, yet the truth remains that lasting, substantial transformation doesn't transpire overnight. It emerges from an unwavering dedication to continuous growth and self-improvement.

Consider the story of John, a character who encapsulates the core principle of 1% improvement. John aspired to become a writer but consistently found himself daunted by the monumental task of crafting an entire book. He consciously embraced the journey of perpetual growth and committed himself to writing just one page daily. Initially, this daily output might have seemed inconsequential, but it became a customary practice as time unfolded. Weeks turned into months, and John held a completed manuscript before he knew it.

John's narrative isn't a solitary one. It's a testament to the power of consistent, incremental advancement. His journey mirrors the notion that seemingly minor daily enhancements, even if they appear trifling in the short term, can amass into something extraordinary over time. This is a principle that finds relevance in almost any endeavor.

Whether one's aspirations involve personal development, physical fitness, career progression, or skill refinement, grasping the concept of 1% improvement can be a transformative game-changer. The voyage of continuous growth doesn't involve the pursuit of perfection; it centers on pursuing progress. It acknowledges that perfection remains an elusive ideal, but we draw nearer to our dreams by taking modest steps each day.

The philosophy of 1% improvement doesn't limit itself to self-improvement. It's a mindset that holds value for organizations, businesses, and entire societies. As individuals can gain from small, sustained changes, so can larger entities. In the corporate sphere, for instance, a dedication to persistent enhancement in processes and products can usher in heightened efficiency, innovation, and competitiveness.

To welcome the voyage of continuous growth is to embrace the understanding that the course to success doesn't always unfold linearly. It acknowledges the presence of setbacks and trials, perceiving them as opportunities for learning and adaptation. It's an acknowledgment that each stride forward brings us nearer to our aspirations, no matter how slight.

In the previous segments of this book, we delved into pragmatic approaches for integrating the spirit of 1% improvement into various dimensions of life. We discussed the art of setting attainable goals, maintaining motivation, and surmounting the inevitable obstacles strewn along the journey of self-improvement. This roadmap guides all those seeking to harness the potency of systematic, incremental progress on their quest toward a more gratifying and successful existence.

Self-improvement and continuous growth are naturally linked to the concept of minor improvements and the idea of achieving 1% progress each day. These twin principles provide a roadmap for individuals to foster lasting change. Let's explore how this improvement can be achieved through self-improvement and continuous growth.

SETTING CLEAR GOALS

The first step toward self-improvement and continuous growth is setting clear, well-defined goals. These objectives serve as beacons, guiding our actions and decisions. The philosophy of 1% improvement encourages us to break down these goals into smaller, achievable targets. Defining specific milestones creates a sense of direction and purpose, allowing us to measure our progress effectively.

EMBRACING CONSISTENCY

Continuous growth is driven by consistency. Small, daily improvements become ingrained in our routines, becoming habits that propel us toward our goals. While seemingly minor, these consistent efforts accumulate over time, ultimately leading to significant advancements in our personal and professional lives.

CULTIVATING A GROWTH MINDSET

A growth mindset is the foundation of self-improvement and continuous growth. It's the belief that our abilities and intelligence can be developed through dedication and hard work. By adopting this mindset, we see challenges as opportunities for learning and growth. Embracing a growth mindset fosters resilience in the face of setbacks and fuels our determination to pursue incremental progress.

LEARNING FROM SETBACKS

In the journey of self-improvement, setbacks are inevitable. However, they are not roadblocks but stepping stones to growth. Continuous growth encourages us to view failures and obstacles as valuable learning experiences. By examining these setbacks, we gain insights that help us adjust our strategies, refine our goals, and progress even further.

SEEKING FEEDBACK AND MENTORSHIP

Feedback from others and mentorship play crucial roles in our quest for self-improvement. Constructive criticism and guidance from mentors can give us valuable insights and perspectives. We can refine our 1% improvement approach and make informed adjustments through these external influences.

ADAPTING TO CHANGE

Continuous growth acknowledges that the world is in a state of constant flux. To stay relevant and thrive, we must embrace change. Whether in personal relationships or professional endeavors, adaptability is essential. The philosophy of 1% improvement encourages us to remain flexible and responsive to environmental shifts.

CELEBRATING MILESTONES

As we journey toward our goals, it's important to celebrate the milestones we achieve along the way. Recognizing and acknowledging our progress provides a sense of accomplishment and fuels our motivation to continue. These celebrations remind us of the power of small improvements and keep us on track for continued growth.

EXPANDING BEYOND THE SELF

The principles of self-improvement and continuous growth extend beyond personal development. They are tools for driving change in various domains, including relationships, careers, and global impact. By applying these principles to our interactions with others and contributions to society, we can become catalysts for positive, lasting change on a broader scale.

In the chapters that have preceded this conclusion, we've witnessed how the combined forces of self-improvement and continuous growth empower individuals to make progress in various aspects of their lives. This combination is the engine of meaningful change, reminding us that we have the power to advance and become the best versions of ourselves continually. Self-improvement and continuous growth are the twin forces that transform ordinary lives into extraordinary ones, and by embracing them, we embark on a journey of perpetual betterment.

BUILDING A BETTER WORLD

"The best way to predict the future is to create it.
—Peter Drucker

As we embark on self-improvement, it's vital to remember that our responsibility stretches far beyond our development. We don't exist in isolation; we are interconnected with our surroundings, communities, and the broader society. This awareness emphasizes the significance of not only transforming ourselves but also participating in the transformation of our environment and society at large.

The concept of personal and societal transformation represents a dynamic, reciprocal relationship. It underscores individuals' profound impact on their environment and, conversely, how the environment molds the individuals within it. This relation is vital to instigating positive, enduring changes in our lives and the world surrounding us.

In many ways, our transformation catalyzes broader societal changes. By concentrating on self-improvement, we become agents for transformation within our communities and society. The ripple effect of our personal growth radiates outward, motivating those in our vicinity to embark on their journeys of continuous enhancement.

In this book, we have delved deeper into the interdependence of self-improvement and societal transformation. We explored how minor enhancements, goal establishment, and adaptability principles can be employed not solely for personal development but also to effect change on a grander scale. This synergy between the self and society forms the bedrock of significant transformation, reminding us of our responsibility for forging a more radiant, gratifying world for all. As we embrace this shared responsibility, we will discover that our expedition of personal growth is inherently intertwined with the journey of societal amelioration, with each one complementing and elevating the other.

REALIZING POWER WITHIN US

The potential to shape a better world isn't an abstract concept but a tangible reality within each individual. Understanding that this transformation doesn't demand extraordinary feats or immediate, colossal changes is essential. Instead, it results from countless small steps, each contributing to a more significant, positive impact. By comprehending this, we realize our capability and obligation to act as architects of change, diligently working to build a better world one step at a time.

The significance of this realization is profound. It underscores that we need not await sweeping, systemic transformations before we take action. The concept of 1% improvement illustrates that our daily choices, actions, and contributions are the foundational elements for a brighter future. It means that individuals, regardless of their background, age, or circumstances, can actively engage in the process of global improvement.

We must proactively shape our environment and society to establish change one step at a time. By acknowledging the potential for change in our everyday behaviors and decisions, we empower ourselves to address pressing issues like environmental sustainability, social responsibility, and economic equity. Our commitment extends beyond personal well-being to the collective well-being of our global community.

Let's explore practical steps and strategies that can be put into practice to create positive change on both individual and societal levels. These strategies are not theoretical ideals but actionable methods that allow us to take those small, meaningful strides toward a better world.

ENVIRONMENTAL SUSTAINABILITY

Environmental sustainability stands as a foundational pillar in the endeavor to create a better world. It encompasses a broad spectrum of actions, behaviors, and choices dedicated to safeguarding and preserving the natural world, ensuring its continued health and viability for current and future generations. This concept is firmly rooted in the understanding that the Earth's resources are finite, necessitating responsible management to prevent ecological harm and resource depletion.

Resource Consumption Reduction: At the heart of environmental sustainability lies the practice of minimizing resource consumption. This includes reducing energy usage, curbing water waste, and limiting the production of non-recyclable materials. Simple, everyday measures like switching off lights when not in use, addressing water leaks, and embracing recycling contribute to resource preservation.

Example: Installing energy-efficient LED light bulbs is a clear example of reducing electricity consumption and lowering greenhouse gas emissions.

Waste Minimization: The reduction of waste is a pivotal component of environmental sustainability. Endeavors to minimize, recycle, or repurpose waste materials carry significant weight. Practices such as composting organic waste and utilizing reusable products alleviate the strain on landfills and promote a more sustainable lifestyle.

Example: Composting kitchen scraps not only diverts organic waste from landfills but also yields nutrient-rich compost, enriching garden soil and diminishing the need for chemical fertilizers.

Preservation of Natural Habitats: Safeguarding natural habitats and biodiversity stands as a critical element of environmental sustainability. The preservation and restoration of ecosystems and the protection of endangered species play a pivotal role in upholding the delicate equilibrium of our ecosystems.

Example: Collaborative efforts by organizations and individuals to protect the habitats of endangered animals, such as sea turtles or rhinoceroses, can significantly contribute to their survival.

Advancement of Renewable Energy: The shift from fossil fuels to renewable energy sources constitutes a fundamental step in reducing our carbon footprint. Wind, solar, and hydroelectric power represent sustainable alternatives that aid in diminishing greenhouse gas emissions and mitigating climate change.

Example: Investing in solar panels for personal use or advocating for policies that promote the utilization of renewable energy sources decreases reliance on fossil fuels.

Advocacy and Education: Environmental sustainability thrives on awareness and education. Advocacy for sustainable practices and policies and educating others about the significance of environmental protection can lead to the broader adoption of eco-friendly behaviors.

Example: An individual or group may advocate for local policies that ban single-use plastic bags, substantially reducing plastic waste.

Support for Sustainable Practices: Championing sustainable practices across various industries, from agriculture to fashion, can yield far-reaching effects. Opting to support companies that prioritize sustainable production methods encourages environmentally friendly business practices.

Example: Choosing clothing brands that employ eco-friendly materials and ethical manufacturing processes promotes sustainability within the fashion industry.

Carbon Emission Reduction: Carbon emissions play a significant role in climate change. Efforts to diminish personal carbon emissions, such as utilizing public transportation, carpooling, or walking and biking, contribute to a more sustainable future.

Example: Opting for public transportation over driving solo to work allows an individual to reduce carbon emissions and alleviate traffic congestion.

Environmental sustainability hinges on choices that enhance our quality of life and safeguard the planet's intricate ecosystems. By incorporating sustainable practices into our daily routines, we can significantly curtail our environmental impact and create a better world. This isn't just an individual endeavor; it's a collective responsibility capable of instigating profound changes for our planet and future generations.

SOCIAL RESPONSIBILITY

Social responsibility is a potent concept that beckons individuals to grasp their pivotal role in fashioning a better world, one step at a time. It revolves around comprehending the interdependence of our global society and taking purposeful actions to tackle societal challenges, enact constructive change, and contribute to the welfare of communities and the broader world. In the following section, we shall delve into social responsibility, examining its meaning and how it can be integrated into various spheres of life.

Social responsibility encompasses the acknowledgment that each individual's deeds possess the potential to influence society and the environment. It transcends personal well-being, embracing the common good. This acknowledgment underscores that every choice and action, regardless of scale, can contribute to societal enhancement.

Here are some common and easy ways to cater to your social responsibility:

Volunteering and Community Engagement: Engaging in volunteer work and community endeavors is a direct pathway to practice social responsibility. It involves dedicating your time, expertise, or resources to initiatives that benefit the community.

Example: Volunteering at a local shelter, participating in neighborhood clean-up activities, or contributing to food drives exemplify practical community engagement methods.

Ethical Consumer Choices: Your consumer preferences can sway industries and encourage ethical business practices. Supporting companies and products that prioritize fair labor practices, environmental sustainability, and social responsibility is critical.

Example: Opting for products bearing fair trade certification or from companies deeply committed to sustainability and ethical sourcing can negatively impact global supply chains.

Advocacy for Social Justice: Advocacy constitutes an integral facet of social responsibility. Championing social justice issues, increasing awareness, and advocating for change can instigate local, national, and international transformation.

Example: Advocating for policies that foster diversity, equity, and inclusion within your workplace or participating in peaceful protests to raise societal awareness exemplify advocacy.

Education and Awareness: One of the most potent tools for social responsibility lies in education and disseminating awareness. By imparting knowledge, you can inspire others to become actively involved in societal issues.

Example: Organizing workshops or seminars to educate others about pertinent issues, such as climate change, poverty, or human rights, can catalyze increased awareness and action.

Social responsibility initiates a ripple effect. When individuals act responsibly, their actions inspire others to do the same. These small, individual steps amalgamate into collective endeavors that can lead to considerable societal transformation.

For example, volunteering at a local shelter can inspire other community members to follow suit. This offers immediate aid to those in need and prompts more people to partake in community service. Gradually, this collective endeavor can usher in transformative shifts in the community's approach to societal challenges.

Intersection with Personal Growth: Social responsibility and personal growth are intertwined. Engaging in socially responsible actions doesn't only benefit society but also fosters an individual's personal development. It nurtures empathy, compassion, and a sense of purpose, all contributing to personal fulfillment and growth.

Social responsibility constitutes a call to action for individuals to emerge as active contributors to a better world. It urges us to transcend self-interest and acknowledge our obligation to positively influence society, whether through everyday actions or more substantial contributions.

PERSONAL GROWTH AND POSITIVE INFLUENCE

Personal growth and positive influence, intimately connected components, are central to our mission to forge a superior world. They serve as the bedrock for transformation and are instrumental in kindling inspiration and propelling others to partake in this metamorphic journey. In this comprehensive exploration, we shall plunge into the profound import of personal growth and positive influence and their role in the advancement of society.

Personal Growth: At its core, personal growth is the conscious and unceasing journey of self-enhancement, both cognitively and emotionally. It encompasses the development of qualities such as self-awareness, emotional intelligence, resilience, empathy, and a growth-oriented mindset. Personal growth elevates the individual and exerts a far-reaching influence on the community and society.

1. *Empathy and Compassion:* Personal growth fosters attributes like empathy and compassion, which are fundamental for promoting harmonious relationships and constructing a more inclusive, compassionate society.

2. *Resilience:* A resilient individual is better equipped to navigate life's trials, emerging as a wellspring of sustenance and constancy for others.

3. *Self-awareness:* Self-awareness empowers individuals to discern their strengths and arenas for amelioration, rendering them more productive in their interactions and contributions to society.

4. *Perpetual Learning:* A growth-oriented mindset, a pivotal facet of personal growth, instills a culture of ongoing

learning and adaptation, a critical ingredient for societal progression.

Positive Influence: Positive influence entails inspiring others through deeds, expressions, and principles. It is the art of leading by example and spurring those in one's vicinity to embrace personal growth and affirmative change.

1. *Inspiration:* Positive influencers stand as founts of inspiration. They exemplify behaviors, values, and attitudes others esteem and desire to emulate.

2. *Motivation:* By epitomizing personal growth and enhancement gains, positive influencers galvanize those around them to embark on their odysseys of self-improvement.

3. *Support and Encouragement:* Positive influencers afford support and encouragement, bolstering others to vanquish obstructions and stay resolute in their aspirations.

4. *Societal Transformation:* Through combined exertions, the affirmative influence of individuals can engender more expansive societal transformation. It often serves as the spur for movements, consciousness campaigns, and noteworthy societal metamorphoses.

When individuals pledge to their refinement and set the standard through their actions, they stir others to follow suit. The cumulative repercussions of these endeavors can result in a more benevolent, empathetic, and progress-minded society.

Contemplate the narrative of a teacher who embodies personal growth through unremitting learning and a growth-oriented mindset. This teacher's resilience, adaptability, and dedication to honing their teaching methodologies positively influence their students. The students, in turn, espouse personal growth and manifest these attributes in their scholastic undertakings and personal lives. Upon graduating and entering the workforce, they transport these principles, affecting their communities and workplaces. In this manner, a solitary teacher's personal growth and positive influence exert a long-lasting sway on society.

Personal growth and positive influence stand as a summons to action, beckoning individuals to commit to their advancement and to serve as catalysts for transformation within their communities and beyond. They underscore the potential for each individual to be a force for good in society, engendering a superior world one step at a time.

As you've noticed, throughout the pages of this book, we have discovered the practical steps and strategies to nurture personal growth and positive influence, proffering inspiration and guidance on how to wield a meaningful impact. Through these interlinked components, we can contribute to a society that is more empathetic, compassionate, and oriented toward growth. Collectively, we can labor to craft a superior world for all.

COLLECTIVE ACTION

"Alone, we can do so little; together, we can do so much."
—Helen Keller

Collective action is a potent force in driving positive change within society. It involves individuals coming together, pooling their efforts, resources, and influence to address common issues, enact social change, and create a better world. Now, we will delve into the significance of collective action, how it operates, and its profound impact on societal transformation.

Collective action is built on the principle of unity —individuals with shared values, goals, or concerns unite to amplify their impact. It recognizes that while personal contributions are valuable, working collectively generates a more substantial effect.

Amplified Impact: Collective action is like the synergy of individuals working together to achieve a goal. The combined efforts result in a more significant and far-reaching impact than what could be achieved individually.

Leveraging Resources: By pooling resources, knowledge, and expertise, collective action optimizes efficiency and minimizes duplication of effort. It makes the most effective use of available resources.

Diverse Perspectives: Collective action brings together people with diverse backgrounds, experiences, and expertise. This diversity enriches the approach to solving societal issues, fostering innovation and comprehensive solutions.

Process of Collective Action: Now, let's break down the process of collective action:

1. *Defining Objectives:* Collective action begins by identifying common goals, values, or concerns. These objectives become the unifying force that brings people together.

2. *Organizing:* To work collectively, organizations, groups, or communities are often established. These entities provide structure and coordination for the collective effort.

3. *Resource Mobilization:* Collectives pool resources, including financial contributions, volunteers, knowledge, or influence. This mobilization is essential for implementing initiatives and projects.

4. *Advocacy and Awareness:* Collective action often involves advocacy and raising awareness about the issues or causes they are passionate about. This ensures that their message reaches a broader audience.

Collective action creates a ripple effect in society. The positive changes initiated by a collective can inspire other individuals, groups, and communities to take similar actions. This ripple effect is instrumental in promoting awareness and mobilizing additional support, expanding the reach and influence of the collective.

Consider a community that forms a collective to address environmental sustainability. They pool resources to initiate a neighborhood clean-up project, focusing on reducing waste, planting trees, and educating residents about eco-friendly practices. The success of this collective action inspires neighboring communities to launch similar initiatives, creating a movement that spreads throughout the region. This ripple effect leads to a more environmentally conscious society, with each collective contributing to a more significant, positive change.

Collective action is a call to action for individuals to unite and collaborate for the betterment of society. It emphasizes that unity can drive substantial change, creating a more equitable, just, and compassionate world.

We can contribute to a more socially conscious, harmonious, and transformational society through these initiatives. Collective action is a testament to the remarkable results that individuals can achieve when they work together, one step at a time, to build a better world for all.

ADVOCACY AND EDUCATION

Advocacy and education serve as dynamic instruments for nurturing positive societal transformation. They are pivotal in kindling awareness, stoking action, and rallying individuals and communities to tackle critical issues. Now, let's plumb the depths of the importance of advocacy and education, their modes of operation, and the profound imprint they leave on societal metamorphosis.

Advocacy entails actively backing and championing a specific cause or matter, often aiming to sway public opinion, policies, or conventions. It is a conduit for vocalizing change, advocating social and environmental issues, and pressing for action from authorities, establishments, or the broader community.

Within societal amelioration, education represents the progression of instilling awareness, disseminating knowledge, and nurturing comprehension concerning critical issues. It furnishes individuals with the data and competencies for instigating positive change and contributing to a superior world.

Kindling Awareness: Advocacy and education thrust crucial issues into the limelight of public awareness. They cast a spotlight on concerns that might otherwise fade into obscurity.

Empowering Individuals: These tools empower individuals with knowledge, allowing them to make enlightened choices, take initiative, and participate actively in societal enhancement.

Mobilizing Support: Advocacy and education can muster support from communities, establishments, and governments to confront issues, often culminating in palpable transformations and enhancements.

Workings of Advocacy and Education: Let's elaborate on how Advocacy and Education operate:

1. *Issue Identification:* Advocacy and education often commence with pinpointing issues demanding attention. This may encompass societal injustices, environmental worries, or disparities in health and education.

2. *Awakening Awareness:* The inauguration of a campaign to kindle awareness is a pivotal opening move. Advocates and educators brief the public, stakeholders, and decision-makers regarding the issue's pertinence, extent, and repercussions.

3. *Soliciting Support:* Advocacy aspires to garner support by spurring individuals into action. This could entail liaising with legislators, participating in demonstrations, or endorsing pertinent organizations.

4. *Dispensing Information:* Education involves the diffusion of information, often through diverse mediums such as seminars, seminars, publications, and digital media. This enlightenment enables individuals to adopt enlightened choices and engage in purposeful action.

By arousing awareness and aggregating support, they motivate others to morph into advocates and educators, stimulating an echoing influence that cultivates action and change.

Imagine a local environmental advocacy group. They pinpoint contamination in a neighboring river as a substantive issue. To rectify this difficulty, they inaugurated a campaign to boost awareness, organizing workshops and disbursing instructional materials regarding the aftermath of pollution on the ecosystem. Their undertakings enthrall media attention and invigorate residents to pressure authorities into action. Consequently, policymakers earmark river purifying resources, yielding beneficial environmental and communal health consequences.

Advocacy and education stand as summons to action, beckoning individuals to amass wisdom and involvement in pivotal issues and to employ their voices and knowledge to precipitate change. They accentuate that individuals, communities, and establishments hold the authority to impact policies and conventions, augmenting the potential for a more equitable, fair, and empathetic society.

Recognizing the potential for change within ourselves and the world is just the beginning. By embracing these practical steps, we can construct a better world, one step at a time.

YOUR JOURNEY BEGINS NOW

"In a gentle way, you can shake the world."

—Mahatma Gandhi

As we draw near to the culmination of this enlightening voyage through the principles of gradual, step-by-step improvements and their profound effects on personal development, societal change, and positive transformation, we invite you to embark on your unique path of perpetual growth and change. The importance of realizing the potential for transformation within ourselves and society cannot be emphasized enough. This journey commences with self-awareness, empathy, and a dedicated commitment to advancement, and it extends outward, creating a more inclusive and harmonious world for all.

Take a moment to ponder your aspirations, values, and areas for personal development. What do you hope to attain for yourself and your community? Which values resonate deeply with you, and how do you envision translating them into tangible actions?

This reflective exercise serves as the genesis of your expedition toward self-improvement and societal enhancement.

Pledge yourself to make 1% improvements in your everyday life. Acknowledge that significant change emerges from the accumulation of minor, consistent actions. Establish attainable objectives and devise a plan for your personal development. Whether your endeavor pertains to nurturing empathy, championing a social cause, or enhancing a particular skill, each small stride contributes to the betterment of the whole.

Comprehend your potential to wield a positive influence in your community. Embrace your role as a catalyst for change, rousing others through your deeds, principles, and unwavering commitment to growth. Remember that your influence extends beyond your immediate circle, initiating a ripple effect that can enact more extensive societal transformation.

Last but not least, bear in mind that you are not on this journey alone. Seek the support and resources to assist you in your quest for self-improvement and positive change. Communities, organizations, and kindred spirits stand ready to offer guidance, motivation, and practical aid along your path.

We urge you to dedicate yourself to your voyage of unceasing growth and transformation, one slight, gradual improvement at a time. Doing so contributes to constructing a better world enriched by the cumulative efforts of individuals who recognize their potential for change.

Together, we can build a system where each minor yet significant step contributes to a more luminous and promising future for all. Let us serve as the architects of this transformation, constructing a world marked by increased compassion, empathy, and inclusiveness. The moment to take action is now. Embrace the journey of unceasing growth and transformation, and become vital to the positive change our world urgently craves.

INDEX

O

P

Q

R

www.ingramcontent.com/pod-product-compliance
Lightning Source LLC
Chambersburg PA
CBHW030359130626
46549CB00004B/1562
* 9 7 9 8 9 8 8 6 0 3 8 4 9 *